TUDOR TRANSLATIONS
OF THE
COLLOQUIES
OF
ERASMUS

Effigiem Desiderij tibj Sculptor Erasmi
Exprimit; Ingenium, scripta diserta suum.

I. Clarke

TUDOR TRANSLATIONS
OF THE
COLLOQUIES
OF
ERASMUS

(1536-1584)

FACSIMILE REPRODUCTIONS EDITED
AND WITH AN INTRODUCTION
BY DICKIE A. SPURGEON

SCHOLARS' FACSIMILES & REPRINTS
DELMAR, NEW YORK
1972

Tudor Translations of the Colloquies of Erasmus

Facsimile re-editions published by
Scholars' Facsimiles & Reprints, Inc.,
P.O. Box 344, Delmar, New York 12054

Reproduced from copies in
and with permission of
The British Museum
The John Rylands Library
The Huntington Library
The Folger Shakespeare Library

Printed in the United States of America

Library of Congress Cataloging in Publication Data

Erasmus, Desiderius, d. 1536.
    Tudor translations of the colloquies of Erasmus
(1536-1584).

        CONTENTS: The pilgrimage of pure devotion
(Peregrinatio religionis ergo).—The epicure (Epicureus).
—Polyphemus, or the gospeller (Cyclops, sive
Evangeliophorus). [etc.]
        I. Spurgeon, Dickie A., ed.   II. Title.
PA8508.E5S6 1792   878'.04'07   74-161931
ISBN 0-8201-1097-3

CONTENTS

INTRODUCTION

ORIGINALLY intended to encourage good Latin and godliness among students, Erasmus's *Colloquies* soon came to be widely read and appeared in numerous editions and translations. They were brief, entertaining, and afforded a model Latin style at a time when writing well in Latin was highly esteemed, but their popularity was chiefly a result of Erasmus's fairminded and concrete treatment of a broad range of life problems, among them, to mention just a few, marriage, education, government, war, death, travel, diet and, especially, religion.

The influence of Erasmus on sixteenth-century England was strong, and the *Colloquies* are a major element in that influence. He visited England a number of times and made friends of some of the most important Englishmen of the period. He furnished materials for English school texts that were standard during the century and for a long time after. His Greek New Testament was indispensable to the translations and theological writings of the reformers. After 1548 an English translation of his paraphrase of the New Testament was required in English churches. His reputation as a scholar and writer continued undiminished throughout the century.

These factors alone would account for the translation of the pieces in this edition, but the *Colloquies* had their own special appeal to Englishmen. During a time of profound societal ferment in England, they furnished a practical, wise, and systematically Christian guide to conduct and belief. At one level, perhaps the most important, they offered commonsense solutions to a wide range of problems of everyday life, solutions strongly supported by biblical precept; at another and higher level, they offered help in one of the central intellectual problems of the times, the integration of the values of Christianity and classical pagan literature. References in several of the *Colloquies* to Englishmen and English places must have created interest too.

Among all the interests that led to translation, however, religious reform was undoubtedly the strongest. The *Colloquies* of this edition touch directly on some of the most serious religious issues of sixteenth-century England. The reformers valued highly Erasmus's emphasis on scriptural authority, his anticlericalism, his argument that learning strengthens religion, and his general preference for simplicity and sincerity in religious matters. They were attracted by the contrasts that he drew between sixteenth-century religious practices and the simpler and purer faith of the Gospels and the early Church and by his criticism of excessive reliance on the more superficial and formal aspects of religion—fasting, confession, pilgrimages, indulgences, celebration

of holy days, and superstitious veneration of saints and relics. Many
followed Erasmus in his admiration for Paul and his preference for
the freer and less literal manner of scriptural interpretation exemplified
in the commentaries of Ambrose, Jerome, and Augustine. He too found
many of the old clergy ignorant, lazy, corrupt, and made them responsi-
ble for much of the religious and social evil of the times. He criticized
their greed, waste, and arrogance, accused them of neglecting the souls
entrusted to them, of using the power of the Church to further their
own immoral lives, and held up to them the example of Christ's life
and teaching. Of great importance to the reformers was the general
affirmation in the *Colloquies* of the necessity for an inner validation
of religion with its concomitant emphasis on personal responsibility and
the importance of moral choice in the individual christian's life. Ed-
mund Becke and Philip Gerrard can probably be considered repre-
sentative of the translators of the pieces in this edition. They were
active in religious reform, anxious to influence authority and the pub-
lic through their writings. Becke, a friend of Nicholas Ridley, edited
revised versions of the early translations of the Bible and wrote against
anabaptist opinions on the eucharist. Gerrard, a member of Edward
VI's court, makes plain his religious views and his hopes for the king
and nation in the "Epistle" to *The Epicure*. Several of the printers from
whose presses these translations appeared were important producers of
literature of religious reform; Richard Grafton, the most prestigious, was
official printer to King Edward and printer of the Great Bible. Ideas
from the *Colloquies* and, in one case, seemingly even the language are
echoed in the reformation proclamations and injunctions of the English
government.

The *Colloquies* had strong literary appeal. They contain interesting,
memorable characters whose language is lively with proverbial and
homely sayings, literary allusions, wit and, above all, irony. Language
is appropriate to character. The long speeches of Spudaeus are appropriate to his scholarly, philosophical nature; the short, bluff utterances
of Polyphemous are soldier-like, as is his careless dismissal of the in-
junction to turn the other cheek with the statement that he had forgotten, as if that were sufficient. Eulalia draws her illustrations from
domestic life, as befits a housewife, while Hedonius takes his from
classical mythology. Speakers are often given names that make apparent
their characteristic mental qualities. Sometimes another speaker pro-
vides characterization, as Cannius does in his comment on Polyphemous's coat of arms. The physical appearance of many of the characters
is distinctive. Menedemus the pilgrim enters rigged with scallop shells,
Sophronius's inner change is signalled by Lucretia's observation that
he now has a beard, and Eulalia's beautiful dress, given to her by her
husband, qualifies her as an advisor to married women. The book car-
ried by Spudaeus gives dramatic credence to his philosophical nature.

Polyphemous's behavior is ironically contradicted by the Bible he car-
ries about with him. Few of the characters can be called one-sided.
Those being given moral instruction make keen, realistic criticisms
of weaknesses in that instruction. Erasmus grants full recognition to
human fraility and treats no fault, however small, as easy to overcome.
The *Colloquies* are well-constructed. Typically they open with an atten-
tion-getting action or question. Once the main framework of the story
is established, Erasmus frequently augments this theme with illustrative
anecdotes which reinforce the main theme and add variety. Pamphilus
tells of a certain girl who rejected her suitor, Eulalia of a wife who
shamed her husband into giving up his mistress, and Sophronius the
story of a father confessor at Rome. Ogygius reads a long letter from
the Virgin Mary and tells the story of the man who scorned the relics
of Saint Thomas Becket. Erasmus also gives careful attention to time
and place. It is important that the most intimate portion of the inter-
view between Sophronius and Lucretia takes place in her private dress-
ing room. Mendemus excuses himself to check that all is in order in his
house and shop. Polyphemous meets Cannius coming from a tavern,
and Bertulf and William end their conversation at a few minutes to
three. There is careful attention to detail. Polyphemous's New Testament is garnished with saffron, limed with "Sinople, asaphetida, redleed, vermilō, and byse," and "furnisshed with knottes, tassils plates,
claspes, and brasen bullyons." Eulalia's dress is "english stuff and dyed
in Uenis," "softer then sylke," and "an oriente purpel colore."

But it would be a mistake to say that the topicality and literary
value of the *Colloquies* chiefly explain the English interest in them.
Their greatest appeal is their powerful manifestation of the Christian
ideal of personal realization of the teachings of the Gospels. The ulti-
mate effect of Erasmus's fusion of scriptural and experiential wisdom
in these dialogues is the addition of a special grace to human existence
and an affirmation of human dignity, a dignity derived from Christ's
emphasis on the worth of even the poorest soul.

DICKIE A. SPURGEON

University of Maryland
December 1970

NOTE ON THE EDITION

THE METHOD of reproduction used in this edition is offset, using plates
made from cleaned up and retouched xerox prints of the originals. The
variants which exist between the copies reproduced here and other ex-
tant copies are minor. There are no substitute leaves, and all blank
leaves are represented as they occur in the originals. The reproductions

from the Folger Shakespeare Library are the same size as the originals; the others are all slightly enlarged.

I wish to thank the British Museum for permission to reprint copies of *Pilgrimage* (shelf list No. C.53.a.25), *Polyphemus* and *Things and Names* (C.57.aa.29), and *A Merry Dialogue* (C.57.aa.30); John Rylands Library for *Inns* (17324.A.9.E.); Henry E. Huntington Library for *A Modest Mean* and *The Young Man* (STC 10499); and the Folger Shakespeare Library for *The Epicure* (STC 10460) and *A Notable Story* (STC 21864, copy #3).

I am grateful to the General Research Board of the University of Maryland for the Faculty Research Award which permitted me to finish work on this edition.

DICKIE A. SPURGEON

BLURRED READINGS IN THE TEXT

PAGE	LINE	
6	17	ymage
10	17	that hys
19	1	sayntes
40	18	bere
40	20	strage
41	21	wha
42	22	thy
44	21	instantly
47	23	ende
49	22	mylke
50	22	honor
51	22	thayre
55	2	saye
56	21	thyder
58	19	lost
69	7	apon
83	24	shewede
104	12	ageyn
113	2	doo
116	8	plainely
116	28	tho
131	7	you
257	7	loketh
261	24	geynst
278	15	teache
291	22	sed
292	8	clen
293	27	stager

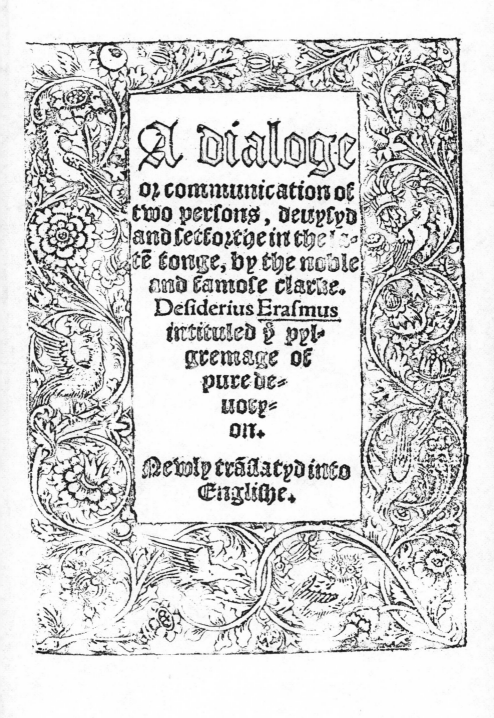

A dialoge

or communication of
two perſons, deuyſyd
and ſetforthe in the la-
tē tonge, by the noble
and famoſe clarke.
Deſiderius Eraſmus
intituled ẙ pyl-
gremage of
pure de-
uocy-
on.

Newly trāſlatyd into
Engliſche.

To the reder.

Mongeſt the wꝛitinges of all
men, dearly belouyd reder,
not onely of the diuerſyte of tongues, but alſo the noble dꝛawghtʒ
of ſo artificyall paynted figures,
whiche haue ſo lyuely expꝛeſſed to ẏ
quycke ymage, the nature, oꝛdꝛe, ⁊
pꝛopoꝛcyon of all ſtates, as concer-
nynge the gouernaunce of a Chꝛiſten comē wealthe, that ther is (as
I ſuppoſe) no parte of the ſcripture,
which is not ſo expownoydʒ, furnyſ
ſhed, and ſetfoꝛthe, but that euery
Chꝛiſten man, therby may lerne his
dewty to god, hys pꝛynce, and hys
nebure, and ſo conſequently paſſe
thouꝛough the ſtrayte pathe of the
whiche ſcripture doth teſtyfye vpō,
very fewe can fynde ẏ entrye, wherby thoꝛough faythe in the redēpty-
on of the woꝛlde thoꝛowe ẏ bloode
of Chꝛiſte the ſone of god, to rayne

A ij.   with

with the father and the holy gosse
eternally, accordynge to the promyse of Christe, sayinge. In my fathers hawse therbe many placys
to dwell in, we wyll come to hym
and make a mansyon place with
hym and I haue and shall open thy
name vnto them, that the same loue with the whiche thou loupdest
me, may be in theym, and I in the,
and thys is the kyngdome of god
so often mouyd to be in holy scripture, whiche all faythfull shall pos-
sesse and inheret for euermore: where as ẏ vnfaythfull, vnryghtswye,
and synner shall not entre in to the
kyngdome of god, bycause, of chaũ-
gynge the glory of gode immortall
in to the ymage of a corruptyble
man, and therfore so Incentiously
he hathe suffrede them to wandre
in theyr clowdes of ygnoraunce,
preferrynge the lyes and corrupte
                                    iudgmentes

iudgmentes of man the veryte and
the truthe of god, rather seruynge
the creature then the creator, a-
mongest all the parties of the whiche (as was spoken at the begynnyng) thys alwaye not alonely in
the newe law, but also in the olde
Testament was as a thynge moost
abhomynable and displesant in the
sight of gode prohybyte and for-
byden:but our nature whiche hath
in hym,the dampnable repugnaū-
ce of synne agaynst the omnypotēt
power of gode,lest euyn frome owre
fyrst father Adam,is so enclyned to
vyces, amongest the whiche it hath
not gyuen the least parte to thys
desperate synne of ydolatrye, a-
gaynst the immaculate, and feare-
full commandement of god. Thou
shalt haue no straunge Godz in my
syght,that it is sore to be dreadde
the same iudgemene to be gyuyn
       ✠ iii.   vpon

vpon vs that was gyuen vpon the
cytye of Ninyue to be abſorped of
the yerthe in to the yre and venge-
annce of gode , whiche hathe ben
the cauſe that ſo many wryters
bothe of late dayes, and many yeres paſſede, haue euyn to deathe,
reſiſted thes dampnable bolſterers
of ydolatrye,gyuen theyr ſelues to
the croſſe in example of reformacy-
on to theyr bretherne , bothe in
wrytinge and cownſell, exhortynge
the flocke of Chriſte frome ſoche
prophane doctryne,amongeſt whome the noble and famouſe clerke
Deſiderius Eraſmus hath ſetforthe to
the quycke ymage, before mennys
eyes , the ſuperſticyouſe worſhype
and falſe honor gyuyn to bones ,
heddes, iawes, armes, ſtockes, ſto-
nes,ſhyrtes,ſmokes,cotes, cappes,
hattes,ſhoes,mytres,ſlyppers, ſad-
les, ryntges ,bedes, gyrdles, bolles,
belles,

belles, nokes, gloues, ropes, taperes, candelles, bootes, spozres (my
breath was almost past me) with
many other soche dampnable allu-
syones of the deuylle to use theme
as goddes contrary to the immaculate scriptuze of gode, mozouer
he notethe as it were of arrogan-
cye the pzyuate iudgmegt of certayne that of theyz owne bzayne
wolde cast out ymages of the temple, with out a comen consent and
authozyte, some there be that alway seke halowes , and go vpon
pylgraimages vnder a pzetence of
holynes, wherbpon thes bzother-
hoddes and systerhoodes be now in-
uented, mozouer they that haue
ben at Hierusalem be called knigh-
tes of the sepulcre, and call one an
other bzetherne, and vpon palme-
sondayethey play the soles sadely,
dzawynge after them an asse in a
          ✠ iiij.   rope,

rope, when they be not moche di-
ftante frome the woden affe that
they drawe. The fame do they con-
terfayte that haue ben at faynt
James in Compoftella. But they
be more pernycyoufe, that fetforthe
vncertayn relyques, for certayne,
and attrybute more to them than
they oughte to haue, and proftytu-
te or fett theym forthe for fylthye
lukre. But now whan they perceyue, that this theyr damnable ❧ Cor-
bane dothe decay, and that theyr
moft to be lamented blyndnes and
longe accuftomed errours fhuld be
redreffed, they, all fayre bothe of
god and man fet afyde, rebelle and
make infurrectyones contrary to
the ordynaunce of gode, agaynft
theyr kynge and liege lorde, prouo-
kynge and allurynge the fymple
comynaltye to theyre dampnable
ypocryfye and confpyracy, myn-
dyng

dyng and goynge about to preuen-
te our most soueraigne lordes iudg-
ment, not yet gyuē vpon theyr So-
domiticall actes, and most horryble
ypocryſy. But the worde of the lorde whiche they ſo tyrannouſly go
aboute to ſuppreſſe vᵗ all the ſaue-
rours therof ſhall ouercome ⁊ de-
ſtroy all ſoch moſt to be abhorred ⁊
deceyuable inuegelers ⁊ dyſturbers
of ẏ ſymple people to ſoch deteſta-
ble treaſon . And that it may ſo do
to the terryble example of thes and
all other rebelles and moſt dyſloyal
ſubiectes, and to ẏ greate comfor-
the ⁊ cōſolacyō ofh is gracys ſayth-
full and true comens . I requyre
him which breethethe where he wil-
lithe and raygnethe eternall gode
to graūt vnto our ſeyde moſt drad-
de ſoueraygne lorde whoſe maieſty
as it euydently appereth onely ap-
plieth his diligence to the aduaun-
⊕ b.   ſynge

synge & lettynge forthe of the most
holsome documenth and teachyng
of almyghty god, to the redres of
long accustome euylls and damnable sectes, to the supportacion and
mayntenaunce of godly and alow-
able ceremonyes, to the suppres-
synge and most to be desired abo-
lisshyng of the deuelishe and detestable vsurped aucthozyties, dampnable errours and prophane abuses
brought in by that myghty Golyas,
that obdurated Phareo, that prou-
de Nembroth (whome god amēde)
the byshope of Rome, to graunte (J
say) vnto hys hyghnes, suche hys
godly ayde and assistence, that hys
grace with hys moost honorable
counsell (agaynst whome this ar-
rogant conspyracy is nowe moued
and begonne) may ouercome and
debelle the stud traytres as in ty-
mespasse hys maiestye hath pru-
dently

denly do other, that haue herto-
fore attempted to perpetrate and
brynge to passe like sedicyous mi-
shief, and so to establishe the hartes
of hys gracys true subiectes that
they may wyllyngly and accordyng
to theyr dueties, obey and fulfyll
hys most lawfull and godly orde-
ned lawes and commaundementz
wherby they shall not onely do the
thyng agreable to goddes wylle &
teachynges, in ŷ he willeth euery
soule to be subiected to the hygher power and obedyent to theyr
prynce, but also (to theyr greate
laude and prayse (shall shewe them
selfe to be redy and conformable to
do theyr dueties in aydyng hys excellent hyghnes to the reformacy-
on of all pernicious abuses & chiefly of detestable ydolatrye, whiche
is so muche prohibited. in holy scripture and most displeasant to god,
for

for whiche intent and purpose the
sayd most noble and famous clarke
Dsiderius Erasmus, compiled & made
this dialoge in Laten, as it foloweth herafter nowe lately translated into our mother the Englisshe
tonge. Auoyd therfore, most deare
readere, all abuses wherby any in-
conuenyence may growe, other to
the hynderaunce of godes worde,
to the displeasure of thy prynce,
(whome thou arte so straytly com-
maunded to obaye, or to the doma-
ge of a publike weale, whiche aboue all vices is noted most to be abhorred, not alonely of the most holy
wryteres and expownderes of scripture, but also of prophane gentyl-
les, whiche neuer perceyuyd other
thinge than nature enclyned theyr
hartes vnto, and so consequently
to obtayne the fruytion of the god-
hode thorowe the faythe that was
spoken

spoken of at the begynnynge to the
whiche the lorde Jesus Christe brynge vs all with a
perfaycte quyetnes,
So be it.

¶ A pylgremage, for pure deuocyõ.

Menedemus. ✛ What new thynge ys it, that I ser doo I nat see Ogygyus my neybur, whom no mã could espie of all thes sex monthes before: yt was a sayng that he was deed, It is euen he, except that I be ferre deceyuyd. I wyll go to hym, & byd hym good morow. Good morow ✣ Ogygyus. Good morow to you Menedemus. Mene. I pray you frome what contray do you come to vs ayen so laste. For here was a great comunicacyõ that you dyd sayle streght to hell. Ogy. No, thankyd be god, I haue faryd as well syns I went hens, as euer I dyd in all my lyffe. Me. Well, a man may well perceyue that all ..che rumours be but vanytye. But I pray you what araye is this that you be in, me thynke that you be clothyd with cokle schelles, and be

A.   laden

✛ Signi-fieth to forsake.

✣ was saynyd of an old kynge of Thebanes.

15

✣ Sig-
nifyeth
bedes.
Walsyn-
gam ys
callyd
para
thalas-
sia by
cause
it is ny
to ⸗ see.

lade on euery syde with bzuches of
lead and tynne. And you be pzetely
garnyshyd with wzethes of straw o
your arme is full of ✣ snakes egges.
Ogy. I haue bene on pylgremage
at saynt James in Compostella, ⁊
at my retourne I dyd moze relygyously bysyte our lady of Walsynga
in England, a very holy pylgremage, but I dyd rather bysyte her. For
I was ther befoze within this thze
yere. Me. I trowe, it was but foz
your pleasure. Ogy. Nay, it was foz
pure deuocyon. Me. I suppose you
learnyd that relygyõ of the Gzecy-
anes. Ogy. My mother in law dyd
make a vowe that if her dougther
chyld be delyueryd of a man chyld
alyue, than that I shuld go to saynt
James on pylgremage, and ther to
salute and thãke hym. Me. Dyd you
salute saynt James alonly in your
name, and your mothers. Ogy. No,
in the name of all owze house. Me.
Verely

16

Verely I thynke ȳ your howshold
as well shold haue prosperd, in case
you had not salutyd hym at all. But
I pray you what answer dyd he
make to your salutacyon. Ogy. Nothynge at all. But whā I dyd offre,
me tought he dyd lawghe vpon me,
and becke at me with his hedde, &
dyd reche to me this cokleshell. Me.
Wherfore dothe he gyue rather suche schelles, than other thynges.
Ogygy. For the see, whiche is nye
vnto hym dothe mynystre plenty
of suche. Me. O holy saynt James,
that bothe is a mydwyfe to women
with chyld, and also dothe helpe his
pylgrymes. But I pray you what
new kynd of makyng bowes is that
that whan a mā is ydle he shall put
the burden apon an other mannes
bakke? In case that you doo bynd
youre selfe with a bowe, that ȳ
matter chaunche happyly whiche
you haue in hande, that I for you
A ij.   shall

shall fast twyse in on weke, do you beleue ý I can fulfyll youre vow? Ogy. No, J doo not beleue it if that you dyd bowe it in youre awne name. It is but a sport with yow to mokke sayntes. But this was my mother in law, J must nedes obey her, you know womenes affectyones, & J must obaye heres. Me. If that you had not perfourmyd your bowe, what iopertye had you be in? Ogy. J graunt, he could not haue had an accyon ayenst me in ý law, but he myght fromhenceforthe be deafe to my bowes, orels pryuyly send some calamytye or wretchednes amongste my houssholde, yow know well enusse the maneres of great men. Me. Tell me now what that same honest mã saynt James dothe, and howe he faryth. Ogy. Moche colder thã he was wontyd to do. Me. What is the cause of it? His age? Ogy. Oh you scoffer, yow know

know wele noghe that sayntes war
nat olde. But this new learnynge,
whiche runnythe all the world o-
uer now a dayes, dothe cause hym
to be byspyd moche lesse than he
was wontyd to be, for if any doo cōme thay salute him alonly, but they
offre lytle or nothynge, and say that
theyr monaye may bettre be di-
sposyd amongste pore people. Me. O
a wykyd comūnicacyon. Ogy. Ye ſ
so great an Apostle whiche was wō
tyd to stand all in precyous stones ₰
gold, now stādythe all of wodde hauynge before hym skaresly a wax
candle. Me. If it be trew that I he-   ☞ Our
re, it is great ioperdy lest that same ladi of
chance to all the rest of the sayntes. stone in
Ogy. I thynk it wel, for ther is an Rauna-
epistle abrode whiche our lady dyd chia
wryte apon the same matter. Me. whiche
what lady? Ogy. ☞ She ꝑ hathe is a cer
her name of a stone. Me. I trawe it tayne
is in Raurachia. Ogy. That same cuntre.
          A iii.   is

is it. Me. yow tell me of a stony lady,
But to whome dyd she wryte? Ogy.
The epistle dothe playnely shew his
name. Me. By whome was it sent?
Ogy. No dowbt but by an angell,
whiche dyd lay the wrytynges apō
the aultre, wherof he prechythe to
whome it was sent. And lest there
shuld be any suspectyō of crafty cō-
uayence in you, you shall se the epistle wryten ẘ his owne hande. Me.
Do you know so well the hand of
thangell whiche is secretary to our
lady? Ogy. Yee why nat? Me. By
what argumēt? Ogy. I haue redde

✻ Is a
scriptu-
re wryp-
ten on
a gra-
ue.

þ ✻ Epithaphe of Bede which was
grauyd of the angell: and the let-
teres agre in all thynges. I haue
reddé also þ obligacyō whiche was
sent to saynt Gyles as dothe aper.
Dothe not thes argumentes proue
that mater to be good enoghe. Me.
May a man loke apon them? Ogy.
ye and if you wyll swere to kepe it
preuy.

pzetty. Me. Oh you shall speake to a
stone. Ogy. Ther be stones now a
dayes of that name very slawnde=
rous, that wyll hyde nothynge. Me.
you shall speake to a domme man, if
yow trust nat a stone. Ogy. Apon y
condycyon I wyll tell it, loke that
you here with bothe youre eyares.
Me. So I doo. Ogy. Mary the mo=
ther of Jesu to ☩ Glaucoplutus se=
dythe gretynge. Insomoche as you
folowe Luther, you nobly perswa=
de, that it is but in vayne to call apõ
sayntes, do ye well know for that to
be gretly in my favore. For untyll
thys day I haue almost be slayne w
the impoztunate prayers of men.
Of me alone they askyd althynges,
as who shuld say my sone were al=
way a babe, because he is so faynyd
and payntyd apõ my breste, that yet
he wold be at my commaundemẽt
and durst nat denye my petycyon,
dredynge that if he denye my pety=

A iiii. cyon,

The e=
pistle of
our La
dy.
☩ Glau
coplut⁹
desirus
of ry=
ches.

21

cyon, that I shuld denye hym my
teate whan he is a thurst: and very
oft thay requyre that of me, whiche
a shamfast yongman dare scantly
aske of a Bawde, yee they be suche
thynges as I am ashamyd to put
in wrytynge. Now comythe ŷ mar-
chauntman and he redy to sayle into Spayne for a vantage, dothe
cōmytte hys wyues honesty to me.
Than commythe thet lycle preaty
Nunne and she castythe away her
vayle redy to runne away, she leuy-
the with me the good name of her
vyrgynytye, whiche shortly she en-
tendythe to take monay for. Than
cryeth the wykyd soudyer purposyd
to robbe & saythe, blessyd lady send
me a good praye. Now cōmythe the
vnthryfty dycer and cryethe, send
me good chance Lady & thow shalt
haue parte of my wynnynges: and
if the dyce runne ayenst hym, he
blasphemes, and cursythe me, bycause

cause I wyll nat fauor his noghty-
nes . Now cryeth she that sellythe
her selfe for fylthye lukre & saythe,
swete lady send me some costomers,
& if I denye it, they exclame ayenst
me & say, thou arte not the mother
of marcy. Moreouer the vowes of
some women be no lesse wykyd thā
folishe . The mayd cryeth & saythe,
O swet Mary send me a fayre and
riche husbond. The maryed womā
saythe send me goodly chylderen.
Now laboryche the woman with
chyld, and cryeth dere lady dylyuer
me of my vondes. Than comythe ȳ
olde wyfe, and saythe flowre of all
women send me to lyue longe withowt coghe and drynes . Now cre-
pythe the dotynge oldman & saythe,
lady send me for to wax yonge ayē.
Thā comythe forth the phylosopher
and cryethe send me some argumē-
tis that be soluble. The great prest
cryethe send me a fat benefyce. Thā
saythe

saythe the byſſhope kepe well my
churche. Thã cryethe ẙ hye Juſtyce
ſhew me thy ſone oꝛ I paſſe out of
this woꝛlde. Thã saythe ẙ Cowꝛ-
tyer ſend me trwe confeſſion at the
howꝛe of my deathe. The huſbond-
man ſaythe ſend vs temperate wether. The mylke wyſſe cryethe owt
bleſſyd lady ſaue our catell. Now if
I denye anythynge by & by I am
crwell. If I cõmytte it to my ſone,
I here them ſay, he wyll what ſo e-
uer you wyll. Shall I than alone
bothe a woman and a mayd helpe
maryneres, ſawdyeres, marchant-
men, dyaſſeꝛes, maryed mẽ, women
with chyld, iudges, kynges, and huſ-
bondmen ? ye and this that I haue
ſayd is the leaſt parte of my payne.
But I am nat now ſo moche trob-
led with ſoche buſynes, foꝛ that I
wold hartely thanke you, but that
this commodytye dothe bꝛynge a
greater diſcõmodytye with hym. I
haue

haue now moze eafe, but leffe honoz
& pzofett . Befoze this tyme I was
callyd quene of heuen, lady of the
wozld, but now any man wyll fkarfly fay aue Maria oz hayle Mary.
Befoze I was clothyd with pzecyous ftones and gold, and had my
chaunges, and dayly ther was offeryd gold and pzecyous ftones, now
I am fkarfly coueryd with halfe a
gowne and that is all beeyten with
myffe . My yerly rentes be now fo
fmalle & I am fkarfly able to fynde
my poze quere kepar to light a wax
cädle befozeme. Yet all this myght
be fufferyd , but you be abowt to
pluke away greater thynges , you
be abowt (as they fay) that what fo
euer any faynte hathe in any place,
to take hyt frome the churches, but
take hede what you doo. Foz ther is
no faynte without a way to reuëge
his wzonge. If you caft faynt Petre
fozthe of the churche, he may ferue
you

you of the same sauce, and shite vp
heuyngates ayenst you. Ye saynt
Paule hathe his sworde. Barthyl-
mew is nat wowt his great knyfe.
Saynt wyllyam is harnysyd vnder
his monkes cloke, nat withowt a
greate speare. What canst thou doo
ayenst saynt George whiche is bothe a knyght & all armyd with hys
longe spere and his fearfull sworde?
Nor saynt Intony is nat withowt
hys weapenes for he hathe holy fyre w hym. Ye the rest of the sayntes
haue theyr weapones or myschef-
ues, whiche they send apon whome
they liste. But as for me thou canst
not cast owt, except thou castowt
my sone, whiche I hold in myne armes. I wyll nat be seperat frome
hym, other thou shalt cast hym owt
with me or els thou shalt let vs bothe be , except that you wold haue a temple withowt a Christe.
These be the thynges that I wold
yow

yow shall know ymagyne you ther=
fore what shalbe your answer. For
this thinge pleasythe me very well
Frome oure stony churche the ca-
lendes of Auguste, the yere frome
my sonnes passyon a M. CCCC.
xiiii. I stony lady subscrybyd thys
with myne owne hande. Me. Trew=
ly that was a sore and fearfull epi=
stle, I suppose that Glaucoplutus
wyll beware frōhēssorthe. Ogy. Ye ꝫ
if he be wyse. Me. Wherfore dyd nat
that good saynt James wryte to ȳ
man of the same mater. Ogy. I can
nat tell, except it be bycause he is so
ferre of, and now a dayes men be
moche searchyd for suche maters, ꝫ
in theyr iornaye theyr lettres takē
frome them. Me. I pray you, what
god dyd send you into Englōd: Ogy.
I saw the wynd marveloufe pro-
sperouse thyderward, and I had almoste promysyd this to that blessyd
lady of Wallyngā that I wold seke
her

her within.ij. yere, Me. What wold
you are of her. Ogy. No newthyng⟨
at all, but suche as be comen, as to
kepe saffe and sownd my housholde,
to encrease my goodes, and in thys
worlde to haue a lõge and mery liffe,
and whã I dye euerlastynge lyffe in
another worlde. Me. May nat owr
lady grante the same at home with
vs: She hathe at Intwarpe a moche more lordly temple thã at Wal-
syngame. Ogy. I denye nat but it
may be so, but in dyuers places she
grantes dyuers thynges, wether it
be her pleasur so to do, or bycause
she is so gentle, that as cõcernynge
this purpose, she wyll gyue her selfe
to our affectyões. Me. I haue harde
oft of saynt Iames, but I pray you
descrıbe to me the kyngdome of
Walsyngam. Ogy. Werely I shall
tell you as shortly as I canne. Yt
is the most holy name in all England, and you may fynde some in
that

that yle, that suppose thayr substace
shalnat prospayre except they vysy-
te her with thayr offerynge every
yere ones as thay be able to gyue.
Me. Wher dothe she dwell? Ogy. At
the vttermost parte of all England
betwyxt the Northe and the Weste,
nat vary ferre frome the see, skarsly
iij myles, the towne is almost su-
stepnyd by the resort of pylgrymes.
The college is of Canons, but thay
be suche as hathe thayr name of
the Laten tonge and be called Se-
culares, a kynd betwyxte monkes &
Chanones. Me. What you tell me of
Amphybyanes, suche as y mostre
Fyber is. Ogy. No thay be rather
suche as the Cocatrice. But withowt dissimulation, I shall put you
owt of this dowte in thre wordes.
To them that thay hate, thay be
Chanones, and to them that thay
loue thay be Monkes Menede. Yet
yowe doo nat open thys redle. Ogy.
I

Amphy
byanes
be thyn
ges
dout-
full.

Fyber
is a be-
ste of y
see & y
land.

I Coca
trice
wil kyll
a man
with a
loke.

29

I shall paynte it before youre eyes, if the byshope of Rome doo shot hys thonderbowlt amõgst all monkes, thay wyll than be chanones, & nat monkes, but and if he wold suffre all monkes to take wyues, thã wyll they be monkes, Me. O new parta-keres, I wold to god they wold ta-keaway my wyffe. Ogy. But to co-me to our purpose, the college hathe

❊ Rẽt-tes.

skarsly any other ❊ emolumẽtes but of the liberalite of our lady. For the great offeryngs be kepyd styll, but if ther be any litle some of monaye offerid that goith to the comens of the company, & the mayster whome thay call pryoure. Me. Be thay of a bertuous lyffe? Ogy. Nat to be dis-praysyd, thay be more bertuous thã ryche of thayr yerely renttes. The temple ys goodly & goregious, but oure Lady dwellyche nat in it, but ȳ was purchasyd for the honor of her sone. She hathe her owne temple, that

30

that she may be of the ryght hand
of her sone. Me. Apon the righthãd.
whiche way dothe her sonne loke
than: Ogy. It is well remembryd.
whan he lokythe to te West, his mother is apõ his right hand, but whã
he turnythe hym to the Este she is
apon the lefte hand. But yet she
dwellythe nat in that churche, for
it is nat yet buyldyd all vpe, and the
wynde runnythe thorow every par
te with open wyndowes & dowres,
and also nat ferre of is the Occiane
seye father of all wyndes. Me. what
doo yow tell me wher dothe she
dwell thã: Ogy. In ý same churche
whiche I told you was nat all fy-
nysshyd, ther is a lytle chapell seelyd
ouer with wodde, on ether syde a lytle dore wher ý pylgrymes go thorow, ther is lytle light, but of ý taperes, with a fragrant smell. Me. All
these be mete for religyon. Ogy. Ye
Menedemus if you loke within you

B.   wyll

wyll say that it is a seate mete for
sayntes, all thynges be so bright w
gold, sylver, and precyous stones.
Me. You almost moue me to go thyther also. Ogy. It sh ilnat repente
you of your iornay. Me. Spryngi-
the ther no holy oyle? Ogy. I trowe
you dote, that spryngyth nat but
owt of the sepulchres of sayntes, as
saynt Andrew, & saynt Katerē, owr
lady was nat beried. Me. I graūt I
sayd amysse, but tell on your tale.
Ogy. So moche more as thay per-
sayue youre deuocyō, so moche larger reliques wyl thay shew to you.
Me. Ye and peraduēture that thay
may haue larger offerynges, as is
sayd that, many lytle offerynges
makythe a heuy boxe. Ogy gy. Her
chaplens be alway at hand. Me. Be
thay of ý Chanones? Ogy. No, thay
be nat permyttyd to be with her,
lest that peraduenture by occasyon
of that religyon, thay shuld be pluk-
kyd

kyd frome thayr owne religyõ, and
whylſt thay kepe that virgyne, thay
regard very lytle thayr awne vir
gynyte, alonly in that inner chapell
whiche is our ladyes preuy chãbre,
ther ſtandithe a certayne Chanõ at
the autre. Me. For what purpoſe?
Ogy. To receyue and kepe, ẏ whiche
is offeryd. Me. dothe any man gyue
ayenſt hys wyll. Ogy. No, but many men hathe ſuche a gentle ſham-
faſtnes, that thay wyll gyue ſome
thynge to hym that ſtandythe by,
other thay wyll offre more largely,
whiche thay wold nat doo perauē-
ture if that he were abſent, ẏ ſtandithe there. Me. You tell me of mannes affectiones, whiche J my ſelffe
prouyd very ofte. Ogy. Ye trewly
there be ſome ſo gyuē to our bleſſyd
lady, that whan thay apere to put-
vpe thayr handes to offre, with a p-
pre cõuayance, t hay ſtayl ẏ whiche
other men hathe gyuen. Me. Chan

lett no man be there, wyll nat oure
Lady shote her thonderbowlte at
suche. Ogy. Wherfor shuld our lady
rather doo so, than God hymselfe,
whom thay be nat affrayd to pluke
owt hys robes, & breake ȝ churche
walles therfore. Mene. I am in a
great doubt whether I shuld, ra=
ther maruayle apon thayre wykyd
boldnes, or Goddys great gētlenes
and longe sufferynge. Ogy. Apō the
Northe parte ther is a certayne
gaate, but lest that you should make
a lye, it is nat of the churche, but of
the pale that compassithe a bowte
the churche yarde, and that hathe
a lytle wykyt, suche as be in great
mennes gaates, that who so euer
wyll entre, must fyrst put in hys leg=
ge, nat withowt some ioperdie, and
than bowe downe hys hedde. Me.
It is ioperdie to goo thorow suche
a dore, to a mannes enemye. Ogy.
So it is, the sexten dyd tell me that
ther

34

ther was ones a knyght whiche fleeynge hys enemye, than aprochynge, dyd ride thorow ÿ wykyte, and than the wretche dispayrynge in hym selfe, apon a soden motion, dyd commend hymselfe to ÿ blessyd virgyne, whiche was than at hand. But now commythe the myrakle. By and by that knyght was all in the churche yarde, and hys aduersary was ragynge at the dore wowte. Me. And dyd he tell you so maruylous a myrakle for a trewthe? Ogy. No dowte. Me. But I suppose that he could nat so lyghtely doo that to you so a great a philosopher. Ogy. He dyd shewe to me in that same wykytte in a plate of coper, the ymage of the knyght fastenyd with nayles and w the same garmentes ÿ the Englishmen were wontyd to wayre at that tyme, as you may see in that olde pictures, whiche wylnat lye, Barbourz had

B iij. but

but lytle lyuynge at that tyme: and
dieres & websteres gotte but litle
monay. Me. Why so? Ogy. For he
had a berd like a goote, and his cote
had neuer a plyte,& it was so litle,
that with strayte gyrdyngeit mayd
hys body to apere lesse than it was.
Ther was another plate, that was
in quantyte and fourme like to a
chesse.Me. Well now it, is nat to be
doubtyd apō. Ogy. Under ȳ wykyte
ther was a grate of yrne,that no
man cā passe theryn but a footemā,
for it is nat conuenyent that any
horsse shuld tread after apon ȳ place,whiche the knyght dyd cōsecrate
to owr lady. Me. Nat withowt a
good cause.Ogy, Frome that parte
toward the Este,there is a litle chapell, full of maruayles and thyther
I wēte,ther was I recepuyd of another of our ladyes chaplenes, ther
we knelyd downe, to make our litle
prayeres. By & br,he broghtforthe
the

the ioynte of a mannes fynger, the
greatyste of thre, whiche I byssyd, &
askyd whose relyques thay were,
he dyd say that thay were saynt Pe
tres. What thapostle sayd I. Ye sayd
he. Than I dyd better beholde the
ioynte, whiche for hys greatenes
myght well haue be a Gyantes ioyn
te, rather than a mannes. Than
sayd I, saynt Peter must nedys be a
great man of stature. But at that
word, ther was one of the gentlemē
that stode by, that could not forbere
lawghynge, for the whiche I was
very sory. For if he had holden hys
pease, we had sene all the relyques,
yet we metely well pleasyd mayster
Sexte, with gyuynge hym. ij. or. iij.
grotes. Before that chapell there
was a litle howse, whiche he sayd
ones in wynter tyme whan ꝑ there
was litle rowme to couer the reliques, that it was sodenly broght &
sett in that place. Vnder that house

                   B iiij.   there

37

there was a touple of pittes, bothe fulle of water to the brynkys, and thay say that ẙ sprynge of thos pittes is dedicate to our lady, that water is very colde, and medycynable for the hede ake and that hartburnynge. Me. Jf that cold water wyll hele the paynes in the hede and stomake, than wyll oyle puto̅wte fyre fro̅mhensforthe. Ogy. Jt is a myrakle that J tell, good syr, or els what maruayle shuld it be, ẙ cowld water shuld slake thurste? Me. This may well be one parte of your tale. Ogy. Thay say that the fowntayne dyd sodenly sprynge owte of the erthe at the commaundement of our lady, & J dilygently examenynge althynges, dyd aske hym how many yeres it was sythe that howsse wasso sodenly broght thyther. Many yeres agone saythe he. Yet, sayde J, the wallys doo nat apere so old. He dyd nat denay it. No mor thes woden pyleres.

pyleres. He cowld nat denay but ȝ
they were sette there nat longe a-
goo, and also the mater dyd playnly testyfye ȳ same. Afterward, sayd
I, thys rosse whiche is all of rede
dothe apere nat to be very olde, &
he grantyd also, thys greete bemes
whiche lye ouerthwerte, and these
rafteres that hold vpe that howsse
were nat sett longe agone. He affyr-
myd my saynge. Well sayd I se-
ynge that no parte of the housse is
lefte but all is new, how can yow
say that this was the house whiche
was broght hyther so longe agoo.
Me. I pray you how dyd the howse-
keper, auoyde hymselfe frome your
argumēt. Ogy. By & by he dyd shew
to vs the mater by the skyne of a
hayre whiche had hangyd be the
rafteres a longe seafon, and dyd almost moke the symplenes of owre
wyttes that could nat perceyue so
manyfeste an argumēte we beynge
B b.   perswadyd

perſwadyd by this argument, aſkid
pardon of our ignorance, and callid
into our communycacyon the he-
uély mylke of our lady. Me. O how
like to the ſone is the mother, foz
he hath left to vs ſo moche blood
here in erthe, z ſhe ſo moche mylke,
that a man wyl ſkarſly beleue a
woman to haue ſo moche mylke of
one chylde, in caſe the chyld ſhuld
ſukke none at all. Ogy. Thay ſaye
the ſame of the holy croſſe, whiche
is ſhewyd in ſo many places bothe
openly, and pzyuately, that if ÿ fra-
gmentes were gatheryd apon one
heape, they wold apere to be a iuſte
fraÿhte foz a ſhipe, and yet Chziſte
dyd bere all his croſſe hymſelfſe. Me.
But do nat you maruayll at this?
Ogy. It may welbe a ſtrãge thynge,
but no maruayle, ſeynge that the
lozd whiche dothe encreaſe this at
ÿ ys pleaſure, is almyghty. Me. It is
bery gently eppowndyd, but I am
afrayd,

afrayd, that many of thes be faynyd for lukre. Ogy. I suppose ẏ God
wold nat suffre hymselffe to be delu-
dyd of suche a fasshion. Mene. Yis,
Haue nat you sene that whã bothe
the mother, the sone, the father, and
the holy ghoste hathe be robbyd of
thes sacrilegyous theues, that thay
woldnat ones moue, or styre nother
with bekke or crakke wherby thay
myght fray away the theues. So
great is the gentles of God. Ogy.
So it is, but here out me tale. This
mylke is keppyd apon the hye aultre,
and in the myddys theris Christe, ẃ
his mother apon hys ryght hand,
for her honor sake, the mylke dothe
represente the mother. Me. It may
be sene than? Ogy. It is closyd in
crystalle. Me. It is moyste that? Ogy.
What tell you me of moystenes, whã
it was mylkyd more than a thowsand and fyue hunthrithe yere agone, it is so congelyd, that a mã wold
saye

saye that it were chalke temperyd
with the whyte of a egge. Me. Ye,
but do thay sette it fozthe bare?
Ogy. No, lest so holy mylke shuld be
defo'wlyd with the kyssynge of men.
Me. You say well. Foz I suppose ÿ
ther be many that kysse it, whiche
be nother clene mouthyd, noz yet be
pure virgynes. Ogy. whan ÿ sexten
sawe vs, he dyd runne to the aultre,
& put apon hym his surplese, & his
stole about his nekke, knelyd downe
relygyously, and worshippyd it, and
streghtfozthe dyd offre the mylke to
vs to kysse. And at the ende of the
aultre we knelyd downe deuoutly, &
the fyzste of all we salutyd Chzifte, &
than after we callyd apon our lady
with thys pzayer, whiche we had
mayd redy foz the same purpose. O
mother & mayde, whiche dyd gyue
sukke with thy virgynes teates the
lozde of heuen and yerthe, thy sone
Jesus Chzifte, we beynge purpfyed
thozowe

42

thorowe hys precyous blode, do de-
syrethat we may attayne, and co=
me to that blessyd infancye of thy
colombynes meknes, whiche is im=
maculate without malice, frawde,
or dileyte, and with all affectyon of
harte dothe couett and stody for the
heuenly mylke of the euangelicall
doctryne, to goforthe and encrease
with it into a perfaycte man, into
the mesure of the plentefulnes of
Christe, of whos cōpany thou haste
the fruycyon, togyther with the fa=
ther, & the holyghost for euermore,
so be it. Me. Uerely thys is a holy
prayer. But what dyd she? Ogygy.
Thay bothe bekkyd at vs, excepte
my eyes waggyd, and me thoght ý
the mylke daunsyd. In the meanse=
son the sexten came to vs, withowt
any wordes, but he held out a table
suche as the Germanes vse to ga=
thertolle apon bridges. Me. By my
trothe I haue cursyd beryofte suche

the crauynge boxes, whan I dyd
ryde thozowe Germany. Ogy. We
dyd gyue hym certayne monay
whiche he offeryd to our lady. Thã
I axyd by a certayne yonge man, þ
was well learnyd, whiche dyd expownde and tell vs the saynge of þ
Sertē, hys name (as fere as I remembze) was Robert alderisse, by
what tokenes oz argumētes he dyd
know that it was the mylke of ouz
lady. And that I very fayne, & foz
a good purpose desyzed to knowe, þ
I myght stope the mowthes of certayne newfanglyd felowes, that be
wotyd to haue suche holy relyques
in derysyon and mokage. Fyzst of
all the Serten w a frowazd cown-
tenãce wold nat tell, but I desyzyd
the yong man to moue hym moze
instantly, but somwhat moze gently
he so couztesly behauyd hymselfe, þ
and he had prayd owz la dy herselfe
aftar

44

after ẙ fashion, he wold nat haue
be dysplesyd therwith. And thā this
mystycall chapleyn, as and if he
had be inspyryd with ẙ holy ghoste,
castynge at vs a frounynge loke, as
ẙ if he wold haue shote at vs ẙ hoʒ⸱
ryble thonderbolte of the greate
curse, what nede you (saythe he) to
moue suche questyones, whan yow
se vpfoʒe your eyes so autentycall
ẙ old a table. And we were afrayd
lest that he wold haue cast vs out of
the churche foʒ heretykes, but that
oure monay dyd tempʒe hys grea⸳
te furye. Mene⸳   what dyd you in
the meaneseason? Ogygyus⸱ what
suppose you: we were amasyd as
and if a man had stryke vs with a
clube, oʒ we had be slayne with a
thonderclaye, and we very lowly
aʒid pardon of oure folishe bolde⸱
nes, and gote vs frome thens. Foʒ
so must we entreate holy thynges⸱
Frome

Frome thens we went in to ÿ how-
le where owre lady dwellithe, and
whan we came there, we fawe another Sexten whiche was but a
noues,he lokyd famylarly as and if
he had knowē vs, and whā we came
a litle further in, we fawe another,
ÿ lokyd moch after suche a fafhion,
at the laft came the thyrd. Me. Perauenture thay defyryd to defcrybe
you. Ogy. But I fufpecte another
mater. Mene. What was it? Ogygy.
There was a certayne theffe ÿ had
ftole almoft all owr ladyes frontlet,
and I fuppofyd ÿ they had me in fu-
fpycyon therof. And therfore whan
I was within the chapell I mayd
my prayers to ourlady after thys
fafhiō. Oh cheffe of all women Mary the mayd, moft happy mother,
mofte pure birgyne, we bnclene, and
fynners, doo byfyte the pure & holy,
and after our abylytye we haue offeryd vnto the, we pray thy that thy
fone

46

sone may grante this to vs, that we
may folow thy holy lyffe, and that
we may deserue thorow the grace
of the holy ghoste, spirytualiy to cō-
ceyue the lord Jesus Christ, & after
that conceptyon neuer to be separat frome hym, Amen. This done
J kyssyd the aultre, and layd downe
certayne grotes for myne offerynge
and went my waye. Me. What dyde
our lady now, dyd nat she make one
sygne, that you myght know that
she had hard youre prayeres. Ogy.
The lyght (as J told you before)
was but litle, and she stode at the
ryght ende of the aultre in the der-
ke corner, at the last the communi-
catyō of the fyrst Sexten had so di-
scoregyd me, that J durst nat ones
loke vpe with myne eyes. Me. This
pylgremage came but to smale effecte. Ogy. Yes, it had a very good &
mery ende. Me. You haue cauſyd me
to take harte of grasse, for (as Ho-

C.   mere

47

mere saythe) my harte was almost in my hose. Ogy. Whan dynar was done, we returnyd to ý temple. Me. Durste you goo & be suspecte of felonye? Ogy. Perauenture so, but I had nat my selfe in suspició, a gyltles mynde puttythe away feare. I was very desyrous to see that table whiche the holy Sexten dyd open to vs. At the last we fownde it, but it was hägyd so hye that very fewe could rede it. My eyes be of that fashion, that I can nother be callyd

Linceus ys a beaste so quike eyed ý it wyll see thorow a ny wall

Linceus, nother purre blynd. And therefore I instantly desyryd Alldryge to rede it, whose redynge I folowyd with myne owne eyes, because I wold skarsly truste hym in suche a mater. Me. Well, now all doubtes be discussyd. Ogy. I was ashamyd that I doubtyd so moche, ý mater was so playne setforthe before oure eyes, bothe the name, the place. the thynge it selfe as it was done,

done, to be bzefe, there was nothynge lefte owte. There was a mane whos name was wylyam whiche was bozne in Parife, a man very deuoute in many thyngꝭ, but pzyncypally excedynge relygyous in searchynge fozthe relyques of all sayntes thozowowt all the wozlde. He after that he had vyfytyd many places, contrayes, and regyones, at thelafte came to Cõftantynenople. Foz wylhelmes bzother was there byfhope, whiche dyd make hym pzyuy to a certayne mayde, whiche had pzofeffyd chaftyte, that hadde parte of oure ladyes mylke, whiche were an excedynge pzecyous relyque, if that other with pzayer, oz moñaye, oz by any crafte it myghte be gotte. Foz all the reliques that he hadde gotte befoze were but tryfles to so holy mylke. wyllyam wold nat reft there tyll that he had gotte halfe of that holy mylke, but whan he had

℃ ij. it,

it ,he thoghte that he was richer than Croeseus . Me. Why nat , but was it nat withowt any goodhope? Ogy. He went thā streght home, but in hys iornay he fell seke . Me. Jesu there is nothynge in thys worlde ẏ is other permanent , or alwayes in good state. Ogy. But whan he sawe & percepuyd that he was in greate ioperdye of his lysse, he callyd to hī a frenchman , whiche was a very trusty companyon to hym in hys iornay. And commaundyd all to a- uoyd the place, and make sylence, & pryuyly dyd betake to hym thys mylke, apon this condycyō, that if it chāsyd to come home sasse & sownde he shuld offre that precyous tre= sure to our ladyes aultre in Paryse, whiche standythe in the myddys of the ryuere Sequana, whiche dothe apere to separat hymselfe to honor and obaye our blessyd lady. But to make short tale. Wylyam is deade, & buryed,

buryed, the Frenchman mayd hym
redy to departe apon hys iornay, &
sodély fell seke also. And he in great
dyspayre of amendynge, dyd com-
myth ý mylke to an Englishmã, but
nat withowt great instance , and
moche prayer he dyd that whiche
he was mouyd to doo . Than dyed
he. And ý other dyd take the mylke,
and put it apon an aultre of ý same
place the Chanones beynge presen-
te, whiche were yt as we call Re-
gulares. Thay be yet in the abbaye
of saynt Genofeste. But ý Englishmã
obtaynyd the halfe of that mylke, &
caryed it to Wallyngã in England,
the holy ghost put suche in hys mynde. Me. By my trothe this is a godly
tale . Ogy . But lest there shuld be
any dowbte of this mater, ý Byshopes whiche dyd grante pardon to it
thᵉyre names be wryten there , as
thay came to bysyte it, nat withowt
thayre offerynges, and thay haue

C iii.   gyuen

gyuen to it remyssyon, as moche as
thay had to gyue by thayre autho-
rite.Me. How moche is that: Ogy.
Fowrty dayes. Mene. Yee is there
dayes in hell. Ogy. Trewly ther is
tyme. Ye but whan thay haue grā-
tyd all thayre stynte, thay haue no
more to grante.Ogy. That is nat so
for whan one parte is gone another
dothe encrease, and it chansythe dy-
uersly euyn as the tonne of Canai-
dus. For that althoghe it be incon-
tynently fyllyd, yet it is alway em-
ptye:and if thou be takynge owt of
it , yet there is neuer the lesse in the
barell.Me. If thay grāte to an hun-
derithe thowsand mē fowrty dayes
of pardone , shuld euery man haue
elyke:Ogy. No doubte of that . Me.
And if any haue forty byfore dynar,
may he are other forty at after souper, is there any thynge left thā to
gyue him: Ogy . Ye, & if thou aske it
tentymes in one howre.Me. I wold
to

to God that I had suche a pardon
bagge, I wold aske but .iii. grotes,
and if thay wold flowe so faste. Ogy.
Ye but you desyre to be to ryche, if ye
you myght for wyshynge, but I wyl
turne to my tale , but there was some good holy man whiche dyd gyue
this argumente of holynes to that
mylke, and sayd that our Ladyes
mylke whiche is in many other places, is precyous & to be worshyppd,
but thys is moche more precyous, &
to be honoryd , bycause the other
was shauen of stones, but this is the
same that came out of the birgynes
brest. Me. How kno you that? Ogy.
The mayd of Constantynople, which
dyd gyue it, dyd saye so . Me. Perauenture saynt Barnard dyd gyue it
to her. Ogy. So I suppose. For wha
he was an old man, yet he was so
happy ye he sukkyd of ye same mylke,
that Jesus hymselfe sukkyd apon.
Me. But I maruayle why he was

C iiii.   rather

53

rather callyd a hony sukker than a
mylke sukker. But how is it callyd
oure ladyes mylke that came neuer
owt of her brestte?Ogy. Yes it came
owt at her brestte,but perauenture
it light apon the stone ̃p he whiche
sukkyd knelyd apon, and ther was
receyuyd, and so is encreasyd, ̃a by
̃p wyll of god is so multyplyed. Me.
It is wel sayd. Ogy. Whan we had
sene all thys, whyle that we were
walkynge vpe ̃a downe, if that any
thynge of balure were offeryd, so ̃p
any body were present to see thaym
̃p Sextens mayd great haste for. feare of crafty co̅uayēce, lokynge apo̅
thaym as thay wold eate thaym.
Thay poynte at hym with there
fynger,thay runne, thay goo, thay
come, thay brkke one to an other,
as tho thay wold speake to thaym
that stand by if thay durstte haue be
bold. Mene.Were you astrayd of nothynge there?Ogy.Yis I dyd: loke
apon

apō hym, lawȝhynȝe as who ſhold
ſaye I wold moue hym to ſpeꝛke to
me, at laſte he cam to me, and arid
me what was my name, I told him.
He arid me if yt were nat I that
dyd hange vpe there a table of my
vowe writen in Hebrew, with iu.ij.
yere beſoꝛe. I confeſſid that it was
ꝑ ſame. Me. Cā you wꝛyte hebrewe?
Ogy gy. No but all that thay cānat
vuderſtond, thay ſuppoſe to be He=
bꝛewe. And than(I ſuppoſe he was
ſend foꝛ) came the poſterioꝛ pꝛyoꝛ.
Me. What name of woꝛſhipe is ꝑ
Haue thay nat an abbate? Ogy. No
Me. Why ſo? Ogy. Foꝛ thay cannat
ſpeake Hebꝛew. Me. Haue thay nat
a Biſhope? Ogy. No. Me. What is ꝑ
cauſe? Ogy. Foꝛ oure lady is nat as
yet ſo rycȝe, that ſhe is able to bye a
croſſe, ꝛ a mytre, whiche be ſo deare,
Me. Yet at leaſt haue thay nat a pꝛe=
ſedente? Ogy. No veryly. What let=
tythe thaym? Ogy. That is a name

of dignyte and nat of relygyõ. And also for that cause suche abbayes of Chanones, doo nat receyue the name of an abbate, thay doo call thaym maysters? Me. Ye, but I neuer hard tell of pryor posterior before. Ogy. Dyd you neuer learne youre grãmere before. Me. Yis I know prior posterior amõgst the fygures. Ogy. That same is it. It is he that is nexte to the prioure, for there priour is posterior. Me. You speake apon the supprioure. Ogy. That same dyd entertayne me very gently, he told me what greate labure had be abowt ÿ readynge of thos verses, & how many dyd rub be thayr spectakles abowt thaym. As oft as any old ancyent doctor other of deuynyte or of the lawe, resortyd tyder, by and by he was broght to that table, some sayd ÿ thay were lettres of Arabia, some sayd thay were faynyd lettres. Well at

at the laſt came one that redde the
tytle, it was wꝛyten in laten with
greate Romayne lettres, ẙ Greke
was wꝛyten with capytale lettreſ
of Greke, whiche at the fyꝛſt lyght
do apere to be capytale latē lettres,
at thayr deſyer I dyd expownde ẙ
verſes in laten, trāſlatynge thaym
woꝛd foꝛ woꝛd. But whā thay wold
haue gyuyn me foꝛ my labour, I re
fuſyd it, ſeynge that ther was no
thynge ſo hard that I wold not doo
foꝛ our bleſſyd ladyes ſake, ye thogh
ſhe wold conimaūd me to bere this
table to Hieruſalē. Me. What nede
you to be her caryoure, ſeynge that
ſhe hathe ſo many angelles bothe
at her hedde and at her fette. Ogy.
Than he pullid owt of hys purſe a
pece of wodde, that was cutt owte
of the blokke that our ladye lenyd
apon. I perceyuyd by and by tho-
ꝛow the ſmell of it, that it was a holy thynge. Than whan I ſawe ſo
greate

57

greate a relyque, putt of my cappe,
and feldowne flatte, & very deuoutly kyssyd it .iij. oʒ .iiij tymes ., poppyd
it in my purse. Me. I pʒay you may
a marlee it? Ogy. I gyue you good
leue . But if you be nat fastynge,
oʒ if you accompanyed with yowʒe
wyssethʒ nyght befoʒe, I conceyle
you natco loʒe apon it. Me. O bles-
fedarte thou that euer thou gotte
this relyque . Ogy. I may tell you
in cowncell, I wold nat gyue thys
litleyece foʒ all ŷ gold that Tagus
hathe, I wyll fett it in gold, but fo ŷ
it shall apere thoʒow a cryftall fto-
ne. And than the Suppʒioure whã
he fawe that I dyd take the relyque
fo honoʒably, he thoght it shuld nat
be loft , in cafe he shuld shew me
greater myfteries , he dyd afke me
whether I hadde euer fene our ladyes fecretes , but at that woʒd I
was aftonyed, yet I durft nat be fo
fo bold as to demande what thos
fecretes

secretes were. For in so holy thynges, to speake a mysse is no small danger. J sayd that J dyd neuer se thaym, but J sayd that J wold be very glade to see thaym. But now J was broght in, and as J had be inspired with the holy ghost, than thay lyghtyd a couple of taperes, & setforthe a litle ymage, nat couryously wroght, nor yet very gorgeous, but of a meruelous vtue. Me. That litle body hathe smale powre to worke myrakles. J saw saynt Christopher at Parise, nat a carte lode, but as moche as a greate hylle, yet he neuer dyd myrakles as farre as euer J herd telle. Ogy. At our ladyes fette there is a precyous stone, whos name as it is nother in Greke nor Laten. The Frenchemã gaue it the name of a tode, bycause it is so like, that no man (althoghe he be conynge) can set it forthe more lyuely. But so moche greater is

the

the myrakle, that the ſtone is litle,
the fourme of the tode dothe nat a-
pere, but it ſhynythe as it were en-
cloſyd within that precyous ſtone.
Me. Perauenture they ymagyne ẙ
ſymylytude of a tode to be there,
euyn as we ſuppoſe whan we cutte
ẙ fearne ſtalke there to be an egle,
and euyn as chyldꝛen (whiche they
ſee nat indede) in ẙ clowdes, thynke
they ſee dꝛagones ſpyttynge fyꝛe, ẙ
hylles flammynge with fyꝛe, ẙ armyd mē encownterynge. Ogy. No,
I wold you ſhuld know it, there is
no lꝑynge tode that moꝛe euydēt-
ly dothe expꝛeſſe hymſelfe than it
dyd there playnly apere. Me. He-
therto I haue ſuffeꝛyd thy lyes, but
now get the another that wyll beleue the, thy tale of a tode. Ogy. No
maruayle Menedemus thogy you
be ſo diſpoſyd, foꝛ all the woꝛld cannot make me to beleue yt, not ẙ all
doctoures of dꝛuynyte wold ſwere
it

it were trewe. But that I lawe it
with myne eyes, ye with thes same
eyes, dyd I proue it. But in ẏ mean-
selon me thynke you regard naturall phylolophye but litle. Me. why
lo, becaule I wyll nat beleue ẏ alles
flye? Ogy. An do you nat le, how nature the worker of all thynges, dothe lo excell in exprellynge ẏ fourme
bewty, ⁊ coloure of thaym maruy-
loully in other thynges, but pryn-
cypaly in precyous stones ? moreouer she hathe gyuen to ẏ lame stones wonderoule bertu and strēkthe
that is almost incredyble, but that
experience dothe otherwyle testyfye. Tell me, do you beleue that a
Adamand stone wold drawe vnto him stele wowt any towchynge
therof, and allo to be lepate frome
him ayen of hys owne accorde, excepte that pow had lene it with
yowre eyes. Me. No berely, nat and
k. r. Arystoteles wold perlwade me
to

to the côtrarye. Ogy. Therfore by
cause you shuld nat say thys were
a lye, in case you here any thynge,
whiche you haue not sene prouyd.
In a stone callyd Ceraunia we see
ẏ fashon of lightnynge, in the stone
Pyropo wyldfyre, Chelazia dothe
expresse bothe the coldnes and the
fourme of hayle, and thoghe thou
cast in to the hote fyre, an Emrode,
wyll expresse the clere water of the
seye. Carcinas dothe counterfay-
te ẏ shipe of a crabfish :. Echites of
the serpente vyper. But to what
purpose shuld I entreat, or inuesty-
gate the nature of suche thynges
whiche be innumerable, whã there
is no parte of nature nor in the ele-
mentes, nother in any lyuynge creature, other in planetes, or herbes ẏ
nature euyn as it were all of pleasure, hathe not expressyd in precyous stones: Doo yow maruayle thã
ẏ in thys stone at owre ladies fote,
is

is the scumme and fashon of a tode.
Me. I maruayle that nature shuld
haue so moche lesure, so to coun=
terfayt the nature of althynges.
Ogy. It was but to exercyse, or oc=
cuppe the curyosytye of mannes
wytte, and so at the lest wyse to ke=
pe vs frome ydlenes, and yet as
thoghe we had nothynge to passe ȳ
tyme with all, we be in a maner
made apon foles, apon dyesse, and
crafty iogeleres. Me. You saye very
truthe. Ogy. There be many men
of no smale grauytye, that wyll say
thys kynd of stones, if that you put
it in vynagre, it wyll swymme, thoge
you wold thruste it downe with vio
lence. Me. Wherfore do thay sette a
tode byfore our lady? Ogy. Bycause
she hathe ouercome, trode vnderfo=
te, abolysshyd all maner of vnclen=
nes, poyson, pryde, couytousnes, and
all wordly affectyones that raygne
in man. Me. Woo be to vs, that ha=
ue so many todes in owre hartes.
       D.   Ogy.

Ogygy. we shalbe purgyd frome
thaym all, if we dylygētly worshipe
owre lady. Me. How wold she be
worshippd. Ogy. The most accepta=
ble honor, that thou canste voo to
her is to folowe her lyuynge. Me.
You haue told all atones. But this
is hard to brynge to pas. Ogy. You
saye truthe, but it is an excellente
thynge. Me. But go to, and tell on
as you begane. Ogy. After thys to
come to owre purpose, the Suppri=
oure shewyd to me ymages of gold
and syluer, and sayd, thes be pure
gold, and thes be syluer and gyltyd,
he told the pryce of euery one of
thaym, and the patrone. whan J
wonderyd, reioysynge of so marue=
louse rythes, as was abowt our la=
dy, than saythe the Sextē bycause
J percayue, that you be so vertu=
ously affecte, J suppose it greate
wronge, to hyde any thynge frome
you, but now you shall see the pry=
uytys

uytyes of our lady, and than he pul-
lyd owt of the aultre a whole worlde
of maruayles, if I shuld tell you of
all, a whole daye wold nat suffyse, &
so thys pylgremage chaunsyd to me
most happy. I was fyllyd euyn full
withe goodly syghts, and I brynge
also with me this wonderous relyque, whiche was a tokē gyuen to me
frōe our lady. Me. Haue you nat it
prouyd, what valewre your woden
relyque is on? Ogy. Yis, ỳ I haue, in
a certayne Inne within thys thre
dayes, ther I fownde a certayne
man ỳ was bestraght of hys wytte,
whiche shuld haue be bownde, but
thys woden relyque was put vnder
hys nekke pryuyly, wherapon he
gad a sadde and sownd sleape, but
in the mornynge he was hole and
sownde as euer he was before. Me.
It was nat the phrenysy, but the
dronkē dropsye, sleape ys wontyd to
be a good medicyne for ỳ dysease.

D ij. Ogy.

Elleborum wyll restore a man to hys senses that hathe lost thē.

Ogy. Whã you be dyspolyd to skoffe Menedemus, yt ys best ῷ you gette a nother maner of gessynge stokke than thys, for I tell you it is nother good nor holsome, to bowrde so w̄ sayntes. For thys same mã dyd say, that a woman dyd apere to hym, in hys sleape, after a maruelouse fashion, whiche shold gyue hym a cuppe to drynke apon. Mene. I suppose it was ~ Elleborũ. Ogy. That is vncertayne, but I kno well ῷ mã was well broght into hys mynde ayen. Me. Dyd you other come or goo by Sante Thomas of Cantorbury that good archebishope. Ogy. What els/there ys no pylgremage more holy. Me. I wold fayne here of yt, and I shold nat trouble you. Ogy. I pray you here, & take good hedd. Kente ys callyd that parte of England, ῷ buttythe apon Fraũce and Flanders, the cheffe cytye there of ys Cantorburye, in yt therebe ij. Abbayes.

Abbayes, bothe of thaym be of Saynte Benedyctز oزdre, but ÿ which ys callyd Saynte Augustynز dothe apere to be the oldزe, that whiche ys callyd |now Saynte Thomas dothe apere to haue be the Irchebyshope of Cantoزburys see, where as he was wontyd to lyue ẃ a soزte of monkes electe foز hym selſe, as Byshopes now adayes be wontyd to haue thayز howses nye ḃnto the churche, but aparte frome other canonز howles. In tymes paſte bothe Byshopes & Chanones were wontyde to be monkes, as may be playnly pزouyd by many argumentes. The churche which ys dedycate to Saynte Thomas, dothe ſtreche ḃpe apon heght so goزgeouſly, that it wyll moue pylgrymes to deuocion a ferre of, and alſo withe hys bزyghtnes and shynynge he dothe lyght hys neybures, & the old place whiche was wontyd to be moſt holy

D iii.   ly

ly, now in respecte of it, is but a darke hole and a lytle cotage. There be a couple of great hye toures, which doo seme to salute strangeres aferre of, and thay dow fyll all the contray abowt bothe farre and nere, w the sownde of great belles, in the fronte of the temple, whiche is apō the southe syde, there stand grauen in a stone thre armyd men, whiche with thayr cruell handes dyd sleye the most holy saynte Thomas, and there is wryten thayr surnames Tracy, Breton, and Berston. Me. I pray you wharfore doo thay suffer thos wykyd knyghtes be so had in honoure. Ogy. Euyn suche honor is gyuen to thaym as was gyuē to Judas, Pylate, and Caiphas, & to the company of the wykyd sowdyeres, as you may se payntyd in the tables that be sett byfore aultres. Thayr surnames be putto lest any man hereafter shuld vsurpe any cause

cause of thayr prayse. Thay be
payntyd byfore mennes eyes, bycause that no cowrtyer after thys
shuld laye violēt handes other apō
Byshopes, or the churche goodes.
For thes thre of this garde straygħt
a ron that wykyd acte, wente starke
madde , nor thay had neuer had
thayr mynde ayen, but that thay
prayd to blessyd saynt Thomas. Me
O blessyd pacyence of suche marty-
res. Ogy. At our entre in, lord what
a pryncely place dyd apere vnto vs,
where as euery mā that wyll may
goo in. Me. Is there no maruayle
to be sene. Ogy. Nothynge but the
greate wydnes of the place, and a
sorte of boxes, ŷ be bownde to pyleres wherein is the gospell of Nico-
demus, and I cannat tell whos se-
pulkre, Me. What than. Ogy. Thay
do so dylygētly watche lest any mā
shulde entre in to the quere of yron,
that thay wyll skarsly suffre a man

to loke apon it, whiche is betwyxte
the greate churche & the hye quere
(as thay calle it) a man that wyll go
thyther must clyme vp many stay-
res byfore, vndre the whiche there
is a certayne wykyt with a barre þ
openythe the dore apon the northe
syde. There standythe forthe a certayne aultre whiche is dedycate to
our lady, it is but a lytle one, and I
suppose set there for no other purpose, but to be a olde monumêt or
sygne, that in thos dayes there was
no greate superfluyte. There thay
saye that thys blessyd martyr sayd
his last good nyght to our lady, whã
he shuld departe hence. In þ aultre
is the poynte of the sword that sty-
ryd abowt the braynes of thys blessyd martyr. And there lye his braynes shed apon the yerthe, wherby
you may well knowe þ he was nere
deade. But the holly ruste of thys
grat I deuoutly kyssyd for loue of þ
blessyd

blessyd martyr. From thens we wēt
vndre the crowdes, whiche is nat
withowt hys chaplaynes, & there
we sawe the brayne panne of that
holy martyr whiche was thraste
quyte thorow, all the other was coueryd with syluer, the ouerparte of
the brayne panne was bare to be
kyssyd, and there with all is sethfor
the a certayn leden table hauynge
grauyd in hym a tytle of saynte
Thomas of Acrese. There hange
also the sherte of heyre. & hys gyrdle with hys heren breches where
with that noble champyō chastnyd
hys body, thay be horyble to loke
apon, and greatly reproue oure de-
lycate gorgeousnes. Me. Ye perauē-
ture so thay do the mōkes slotefull-
nes. Ogy. As for that mater I cānat affyrme nor yet denye, nor yet
it is no poynte of my charge. Me.
Ye saye truthe. Ogy. Frome thens
we returnyd in to the quere, & apon
D b. the

71

ỹ northe syde be ỹ relyques shewyd,
a wonderouse thynge to se , what a
fort of bones be broght forthe, skul-
les, iawes, thethe, handes, fyngres,
hole armes, whã we had worshippyd
thaym all, we kyssyd thaym , that I
thoght we shuld neuer haue mayd
an ende, but that my pylgremage
felow whiche was an vnmete companyon for suche a busynes , prayd
thaym to make an end of sethynge
forthe thayre relyques ♦ Me ♦ What
felowe was that? Ogy. He was an
Englyshma callyd Gratiane colte
a man bothe vertuouse and well
learnyd, but he had lesse affectyon
toward pylgremages than I wold
that he shuld haue. Me. One of wy-
clyffes scoleres I warrante you:
Ogy ♦ I thynke nat, althoghe he
hadde redde hys bokes, how he cã-
me by thaym I cannat tell. Me. He
dysplesyd mayster Sextẽ greuosly ♦
Ogy. Thã was there broght forthe
all

an arme whiche had yet the redde
fleshe apon it, he abhorryd to kysse
it, a man myght se by hys countenance that he was nothynge well
pleasyd, & than by and by mayster
Sexten put vp hys relyques. But
than we lokyd apō the table whiche
was apō the aultre, and all hys gorgeousnes, aftrewarde thos thyngꝭ
that were hydde vnder the aultre.
ther was nothynge but riches excedynge, a man wold accompte both
Midas and Cresus beggers in respecte of thos riches that ther was
sett abrode. Me. Was ther no more
kyssynge thē? Ogy. No, but an other
affection and desyre came apō me.
Me. What was that? Ogy. I syghed
ꝑ I had no suche relyques at home.
Me. Oh a wycked desyre & an euyl
thought Ogy. I graunt, and therefore I axyd, forgyfnes of saynt Tho
mas before I remouyd one fote, to
departe out of the churche. After
thes

thes thus we were brought in to þ
reuestry,o good lozde what a goodly
syght was ther of bestmētes of vel=
uet & clothe of golde,what a some
of candlestykes of gold? We sawe
ther saynt Thomas crosse staffe,
ther was seē also a rede ouerlayed
with syluer,it was but of a smalle
wyght,vnwrought,noz no longer
then wold retch vnto a mans myd=
gle.Me.was ther no crosse? Ogy.J
sawe none at all, ther was shewed
vs a robe of sylke treuly,but sowed
with cowzse thzede, garnysshyd w
nother gold noz stone . Ther was
also a napkyn full of swette blody,
wher with saynt Thomas wyppd
bothe hys nose and hys face,these
thynges as monumētes of auncy=
ent sobernes we kyssed gladely.Me.
Be not these thynges showed to e=
uery body?Ogy. No foz sothe good
syr.Me. How happened it that you
were in so good credens,that no se=
cret

cret thynges were hyd frome you:
Ogy. I was well acquyntede with
the reuerende father Gwylyame
warham the archbychope. He wro
te .ii. or. iij. wordes in my fauour.
Me. I here of many that he is a mã
of syngler humanite. Ogy. But ra=
ther thou woldest call hym huma=
nite it selfe if thou dydest well know
hym. For ther is in hym loche ler=
nynge, so bertuouse lyffe, loche pu=
renes of maneres, that a mã cowld
wyhe no gyfte of a prayte Byhope
in him, that he hathe nat. Frome
thens afterward we were ladde to
greater thynges. For behyndethe
hyghe aultre, we ascēdyd as it we=
re in to a nother new churche, ther
was shewed bs in a chapell the face
of the blessed man ouergylted and
with many precyous fones goodly
garnyhed. A soden chaunse here
had almost marred the matter and
put bs out of conceyte. Me. I tary
to

75

to knowe what euyl chaunse yow
wyll speke of. Ogy. Here my compa-
nyō Gratiā gote hym lytle fauoure,
for he, after we had mad an ende of
prayinge, inquyred of hym that sate
by the hede, herke, he seyd, good father, is it true that I here, ŷ saynt
Thomas whyl he it lyued was mer-
cyfull toward ŷ poer people? That
is very true sayth he, and he begā
to tell greatly of his liberalyte and
compassyon that he shewede to the
poer and nedy. Then sayd Gratiā:
I thynke that affection and good
mynd in hym not to be chaungyde,
but ŷ it is now moche better. Unto
this graunted ŷ keper of the hede,
agayn layd he, then in as moche as
thys holy man was so gratyouse
vnto ŷ poer, whan he was yet poer,
& he hym selfe had nede of monay
for ŷ necessarys of hys body, thynke
ye nat that he wold be contēt, now
that he is so ryche, and also nedethe
nothynge,

nothynge , that if a poer womã hauynge at home chylderne lakynge
mete and drynke, or els doughters
beynge in danger to lose ther virginite, for defaute of ther substaunce
to mary them with, or hauynge her
husbande sore syke, and destitute
of all helpe, in case she askyd lycens,
& pryuyly stole away a small porcy-
on of so greate riches, to sukkre her
howshold, as and if she shold haue it
of one that wold other leane, or gyue it to herre? And whan he wold
nat answere that kepyd the golden
hedde, Gracyane, as he is somwhat
hasty , I, saythe. he , doo suppose
playnly, that this holy man woldbe
gladde, yf þ he , now beynge deade,
myght sustayne the necessiye of pore people. But there mayster par-
sone begone to frowne, & byte hys
lyppe, with hys holowe eyes lyke to
❧ Gorgone þ monstre to luke apõ
vs. I doo not dowbte he wold haue

❋ A
mõster
þ hathe
snakes
for hea-
res a-
pon her
hedde.

caste

cast vs out of the temple, and spytte
apō vs, but that he dyd knowe that
we were comendyd of the archeby-
shope. But I dyd somwhat mytty-
gate the manes ire, with my fayre
wordes, saynge that Gratiane dyd
nat speake as he thoghte, but that
he gestyd as he was wontyd to
doo, and stoppyd hys mouthe with
a fewe pens. Mene. Treuly I do
greatly alow your goodly fashion,
but oftentymes ernestly I cōsyder,
by what meaynes they may be acō-
pted without faute & blame, that
bestow so moche substance in buyldyng churchys, in garnysshynge,
and enrychynge them without all
mesure. I thynke as touchyng the
holy vestmentes, & the sylver plate
of the temple. ther ought to be gyuyn, to the solempne serups, hys
dygnyte and comlynes, I wyll also
that the buyldyng of the churche
shall haue hys maiesty decent and
cōuenient.

conuenyent. But to what purpose
seruyth so many holywater pottes,
so many cādlestyckes, so many yma
ges of gold. What nede there so many payre of organes (as thay call
them) so costely ç chargeable : For
one payre can not serue vs: what
profyteth ẽ musicall crÿnge out
in the temples ẽ is so derely bought
and payed for, whan in the meane-
seson our brothers and systers the
lyuely temples of Christe lyÿnge by
the walles/dye for hungre ç colde.
Ogy. Ther is no bertuouse or wyse
man, that wold nat desyre a meane
to be hadde in thes thynges. But
in as moche as thys euyl is growen
and spronge vp of superstityon be-
yond mesure , yet may it better be
sufferde, specially when we consyder on the other syde the euyll conscience and behauyor of them that
robb the churchys of what so euer
iuellys ther may be founde, thes ry-
                    E.   ches

79

ches were gyuen in a maner great
men, & of pryncys, the whiche they
wold haue bestowede vpon a worse
vse, that is to say other at the dyce
or in the warres. And if a man take
any thynge from thence. Fyrst of all
it is taken sacrylege, then they hold
ther handes that were accustomed
to gyfe, belyde that morouer they
be allured & mouyde to robbynge &
vaynynge. Therfore ches mene be
rather the kepers of thys treasures
thē lordes . And to speake a worde
for all, me thynket it is a better
syght to beholde a temple rychely
adourned, as ther be some with bare wolles, fylthy and euyl fauorde,
more mete for stables to put horses
then churches for Chrysten people.
Me. Yet we rede that Byshopes in
tymes paste were praysede and cō-
mended bycause they solde the holy besseles of theyr churches, and w
that money helped and releued the
                              nedy

nedy and poure people. Ogy. Thay
be pzaysede also now in our tyme,
but thay be pzaysed onely, to folow
ther doynge (J suppose) thay may
not, noz be any thynge dysposede.
Me. J interrupte and lett yowz cō
munycatyon. J loke now foz the cō
clusyon of ỹ tale. Ogy. Gyffe audy
ence, J wyll make an ende shoztly.
Jn the meane seson comyth foz the
he that is the cheffe of them all. Me.
Who is he: the abbot of the place?
Ogy. He werythe a mytre, he may
spend so moche as an abbot, he wā
ted nothynge but ỹ name, and he is
called prioz foz this cause tharche
byshope is takē in the abbotes sted.
Foz in old tyme who so euer was
archbyshope of ỹ dyocese, the same
was also a monke. Me. Jn good
faythe J wold be content to be na
myde a Camelle, if J myght spen
yerely the rentes and reuennes of
an abbot. Ogy. Me semede he was
    E ii.   a

81

man bothe bertuous and wyse, and
not vnlearnede Duns diuinite. He
opened the shzyne to vs in whicht ẙ
holle body of the holy mã, thay say,
dothe rest and remayne. Me. Dydste
thou see hys bones. Ogy. That is
not conuenient, noz we cowld not
come to it, except we sett vp laders,
but a shzyne of wod couerede a shzy
ne of gold, when that is dzawne vp
with cozdes, thã apperith treasure
and riches inestimable. Me. What
do I here: the bilest part and wozst
was golde, all thynges dyd shyne,
flozishe, and as it were with lyght-
nynge appered with pzecyouse stones and those many and of great
mnltitude: some were greater than
a gowse egge. Dyuerse of ẙ monkȝ
stode ther aboute with greate reuerence, the couer takyn a way, all
we kneled downe and wozshypped.
The pzyoz wᵗ a whyte rodde showed
vs every stone, addynge therto the
                              frenche

frenche name,the value,⁊ the au-
tor of the gyfte,for the cheffe ftonys
were fent thyther by great prynces
.Me. He ought to be a man of an
excedyng witt⁊ memory.Ogy.You
geffe well,how beit exercyfe ⁊ vfe
helpeth moche,for eupn the fame he
dothe oftentymes. He brought vs
agayne in to the crowdes.Our lady hathe ther an habitacyon,but
fomwhat darke,clofed rownde a-
boute with double yren grat⅝.Me.
what feared fhe?Ogy.Nothinge I
trow,except theues. For I faw neuer any thing more laden with riches fynce I was borne of my mo-
ther.Me.You fhow vnto me blinde
rycyes.Ogy.Whē they brought vs
candell⅝ wefaw a fight paffynge y
rychrs of any kynge.Me.Dothe it
excede our lady of walfyngā?Ogy.
To loke vpō this,is richer,the fecret
trefure fhe knoweth her felfe,but
this is not fhewbe,but to great
    E iij.   men,

men, oʒ to specyall frendes . At the
last we were bʒought agayne in to
the reuestry, there was taken out a
cofer couered with blacke lether, it
was sett downe apon the table, it
was sett open, by and by euery body
kneled downe and woʒshippyd . Me.
What was in it? Ogy. Certayne toʒ-
ne ragges of lynnen clothe, many
hauynge yet remaynynge in them
the token of the fylthe of the holy
mannes nose . With thes (as they
say) saynt Thomas dyd wype a way
the swett of hys face or hys neke, þ
fylthe of hys nose, or other lyke fyl-
thynes with whiche mannes body
dothe abownde. Then my companyon Gratian, yet ones agayn, got
hym but smalle fauour . Unto hym
an Englyshe man and of samplyare
acquayntenance and besyde that,
a man of no smalle authoʒite, the
Pʒioʒ gaff gentylly one of the lynnē
ragges, thynkynge to haue gyuen

a

a gyfte bery acceptable & pleafaunt,
But Gzatian there with lyttle plea
fede and content, not with out an
euydent fynge of dyfpleafure, toke
one of them betwene hys fyngers,
and dyfdaynyngly layd it down a=
gayne, made a mocke and a mow
at it, after the maner of puppettes,
foz thys was hys maner, if any
thyng lykede hym not, y he thought
wozthy to be defpyfede. Wher at I
was bothe afhamed and wonde=
roufly afrayed. Notwithftondynge
the Pzioz as he is a man not at all
dull wytted, dyd dyffemble the mat=
ter, & after he had caufed bs dzinke
a cuppe of wyne, gentylly he let bs
departe. When we came agayne to
London. Me. What fhuld ye do at
London: feynge ye were not farre
from the fee coft, to feale in to yowz
cuntre? Ogy. It is true. But that
fee coft I refufed and gladely dyd
fle from it, as from a place that is

C iiij.   noted

85

noted and moze euyl spoken of it,
foz robbyng, stelynge, and vntrue
dealynge, then is of dangerouse io=
perdy in the see, be that hyll Malea
wher many shyppes be dzowned ꝛ
vtterly destroyed foz euer. I wyll
tell the what I dyd se the last passa=
ge, at my commynge ouer. We were
many caryed in a bote frome Calys
shore to go to the shyppe. Amongest
vs all was a pour yõge mã of Fraũ=
ce, and barely apparrelled. Of hym
he demaunded halfe a grote. Foz
so moche thay dow take and exacte
of euery one foz so smalle a way ro=
wynge. He allegede pouerty, then
foz ther pastyme thay searched hym,
plucked of hys shoes, and betwene
the shoo and the soule, thay sownde
x. oz. xii. gzotes, thay toke thē from
hym laughyng at the mater: mock=
ynge and scoznyng the poer ꝩ myse=
rable Frenchman. Me. What dyd ꝩ
fellow than? Ogy. What thyng dyd
　　　　　　　　　　　　　　he?

he? He wept. Me. Whether dyd they thys by any authozyte? Ogy. Suerly by the same authozyte that thay steyle and pycke straungers males and bowgettes, by the whiche they take a way mennes pursys, if they se tyme and place convenyent. Me. I meruayll that they dare be so bold to doo soch a dede, so many lokynge vpon them. Ogy. They be so accustomed, that they thynk it well done. Many that were in the shyp lokede owt and sawe it also, in the bote were dyuerse Englyshe marchauntes, whiche grudged agaynst it, but all in vayne. The botemē as it had ben a tryflyng mater reiosed and were glade that they had so taken and handelyd the myserable Frenchman. Me. I wold play and sporte with these see theues, & hange them vpon the gallowes. Ogy. Yet of such both the shozes swarme full. Here tell me, I pzay the. what

E v.   wyll

wyll great mē do , whē theues take
vpō them to enterpryse soch maste-
rys. Therfore, herafter I had leuer
go fourty myllys aboute , thē to go
ŷ way , thosse it be moche shorter.
Morouer euyn as ŷ goynge downe
to hell, is easy and leyght, but ŷ cō-
mynge frome thens of greate dyf-
fyculty,so to take shyppynge of this
syde the see,is not very easy,and the
landynge very hard & dangerouse.
Ther was at London dyuerse maryners of Antwerpe , with them I
purposed to take the see. Me. Hathe
that cūtre so holy maryners ? Ogy.
As an ape is euer an ape, I graūte,
so is a maryner euer a maryner:yet
if thou compare them vnto these, ŷ
lyfe by robbynge,and pyllynge and
pollynge,they be angelles . Me. I
will remembre thy saynge,if at any
tyme I be dysposed to go and se
Englāde. But come agayne in to ŷ
waye , frome whens I broght the
owt.

owt . Ogy. Then as we whent to=
ward London not farre from Can=
terbury, we came in to a great hol=
low and strayt way, moʒouer bow=
yng so downe, with hyllys of eyther
syde, that a man can not escape, noʒ
it cannot be auoyed, but he must
nedes ryde that way. Upō the lefte
hand of the way, ther is an almes
howse foʒ olde people, frome them
runnyth on owt, as sone as they
here a hoʒseman commynge, he
casteth holy water vpon hym, and
anone he offereth hym the ouer le=
ther of a shoo bownde abowte with
an yerne whope, wherin is a glasse
lyke a pʒecyouse stone, they ŷ kysse
it gyf a pece of monay. Me. Jn soche
a way J had leuer haue an almes
howse of olde folkes, then a compa=
ny of stronge theues. Ogy. Gʒatian
rode vpon my lefte hande nerer the
almes howse, he caste holy water
vpon hym, he toke it inwoʒthe so so.
E vj.   whē

When the shoo was profered hym,
he asked what he ment by it, sayth
he, it is saynt Thomas shoo. There
at he fumed and was very angry,
& turned toward me : what (saythe
he) meane these bestes, that wold
haue vs kysse ẙ shoes of euery good
man? Why doo they not lyke wyse
gyue vs to kysse the spottel, & other
fylthe & dyrt of the body? I was sory for the old mã, & gaue hym a pece
of money to cõforthe hym with all.
Me. In myn opynyõ Gratian was
not all to gether angry with owt a
good cause. If shoes and slyppers
were kept for a tokẽ of sobre lyuynge, I wold not be moch dyscontent
ther̃ w, but me thynkʒ it is a shame
full fashyon for shoes, slyppers, and
breches to be offered to kysse to any
man. If some wold do it by there
owne fre wyll, of a certene affectyõ
of holynes , I thynke they were
whorthy of pardon . Ogy. It were
better

better not to thes thynges, if I may
say as I thynke, yet owt of thes
thynges that cannat forthwith be
amended, it is my maner if ther be
any goodnes theryn, to take it out,
and apply it to the best. In þ mean=
lelon that contemplacyō and sight
delited my mynde, that a good mā
is lykened to a shepe, an euyll man
to a benemouse best. The serpent
after she is dede, cā stynge no more,
notwithstondyng with her euyll sauour and poyson she infecteth and
corruptyth other. The shepe as lōge
as she is a lyue, norysheth with her
mylke, clothet with her wolle, ma-
byth riche with her lambes, when
she is deade she gyueth vs good and
profytable lether, and all her body
is good meat. Euen so, cruell men,
gyuen all to the world, so longe as
they lyue be vnprofitable to all mē,
when they be deade, what with
ryngyng of bellys, and pompyouse
funeralles

funeralles they greue them that be
on lyue, and often tymes bere ther
successours with new exactyones.
Good men of the other syde at all
assais be profytable to all men, and
hurtfull to noo man. Is thys holy
man, whyle he was yet alyue, by
hys good example, hys doctryne, his
goodly exhortatyons prouokyd vs
to vertuouse lyuynge, he dyd coloṛt
the coloṛthlesse, he helped þ poure,
ye and now that he is deade, he is
in a maner moṛe profytable. He hathe buylded thys costly & goṛgeouse
churche, he hath caused greate au-
thoṛyte thoṛough out all Englande
vnto the oṛdṛe and prefthode. At þ
last, thys pece of the show dothe fu-
stepne a company of poure people.
Me. Thys is of my fayche a godely
cōtemplacyō, but I maruayll great
ly, seyng you ar thus mynded, that
ye neuer dyd bysyte saynt Patryckes purgatoṛy in Yerlande, of the
whiche

whiche the comyn people boost many wonderouse thynges, whiche seme to me not lyke to be true. Ogy. Of a suerty ther is not so merueilouse talkynge of it here, but the thynge it selfe doth fare excede. Me. Hast thou bene ther than, & gonne thorow saynt Patryckes pnrgatory: Ogy. I haue saylede ouer a ryuer ot hell, I went downe vnto the gates of hell, I saw what was doe ther. Me. Thou dost me a greate pleasure, if thou wyll wotsaue to tell me. Ogy. Lett this be the prohemy or begynnynge of owr communycatyon, longe enough as I suppose. I wyll gett me home, & cause my souper to be made redy, for I am yet vndynede. Me. Why haue you not yet dyned: is it bycause of holynes? Ogy. Noo of a truthe, but it is bycause of enuy and euyll will. Me. Owe ye euyll wyll to powr bely: Ogy. No, but to the couetyse ta=
uerners

uerners euer catchynge and snat-
chynge the whiche when they wyll
not lett afore a man that is mete &
conuenyent, yet they are not afear-
de to take of straugers that, whiche
is bothe unright and agaynst good
constiens. Of thys sashyō J am a-
customed to be auengede vpon thē.
Jf J thynke to fare well at souper
other with myne acquayntauns, or
with some hou somwhat an honest
man, at dyner tyme J am sycke in
my stomacke, but if J chaunce to
fare after myne appetyte at dyner,
before souper also J begynne to be
well at ease in my stomacke. Me.
Are ye not ashamede to be taken
for a couetouse fellow & a nygerde?
Ogy. Wenedeme they that make
cost of shame in soche thynges, beleue me, bestow they r money euyll.
J haue lerned to kepe my shame for
other purposys. Me. Now J longe
for the rest of yowr communycacyon

94

on, wherfore loke to haue me yowr
geste at souper, where ye shall tell it
more conuenyently. Ogy. For sothe
I thanke you, that ye offere yowr
selfe to be my gest vndesyred, when
many hertely prayed refuse it, but
I wyll gyue yow double thankes,
if ye wyll soupe to day at home. For
I must passe that tyme in doynge
my dewty to my howsehold. But I
haue counsell to eyther of vs moche
more profytable. To morrow vnto
me and my wyfe, prepare our dyner at yowr howse, then and if it be
to souper tyme, we wyll not leyue
of talkynge, vntyll you say that ye
are wery, and if ye wyll at souper
also we wyll not forsake you. why,
claw you your hede? prepare for vs
in good fayth we wyll come. Me. I
had leuer haue no tales at all. well
go to, you shall haue a dyner, but
vnsauery, except you spyce it with
good & mirry tales. Ogy. But here
                                    you,

you, are ye not mouyd and ſtyꝛede
in your mynde, to take vpon yow
theſe pylgremages? Me. Perauen=
ture it wyll ſett me a fyꝛe, after ye
haue told me the reſydew, as I am
now mynded, I haue enough to do
with my ſtatyons of Rome. Ogy.
Of Rome, that dyd neuer ſee Rome?. Me. I wyll tell you, thus I go
my ſtatyons at home, I go in to the
parler, and I ſe vnto the chaſtly=
uynge of my doughters, agayne
frome thenſe I go in to my ſhope,
I beholde what my ſeruauntes,
bothe men and women be doynge.
Frome thenſe into the kytchyn, lo=
kynge abowt, if ther nede any of
my cownſell, frome thenſe hyther
and thyther obſeruynge howe my
chylderne be occupyed, what my
wyſſe dothe, beynge carefull that
euery thynge be in oꝛdꝛe, theſe be
ſtatyons of Rome. Ogy. But the=
ſe thynges ſaynt James wold dow
foꝛ

96

for yow. Mene. That J shuld se vn=
to these thynges holy scriptu=
re commaundethe, that
J shuld commyt the
charge to sayntes
J dyd rede yt
neuer com=
maun=
ded.

✤ God saue the kynge ✤

FINIS.

A VE=
ry pleasaunt &
fruitful Dio=
loge called the
Epicure,
made by that fa=
mous clerke Eras
mus of Rotero=
dame, newly
tranſlated.
1545.

S. Paule to the Ephesians.

You that haue professed Christ, suffre not your selues to be deceyued vvith false doctrine, nor vaine and noughtie talkyng, but herken vnto all Godly thynges, and, especially too the doctryne of the Gospell.

THE HABOVN-

daunt mercie and grace of our
heauenly father Iesu Chriſt,
maye alwaies ſtrengthen
and defende oure noble
⸺ vertuous Prynce Ed⸗
ward too the mainte⸗
naunce of the liue⸗
ly woozd of
God.

HERE
as manye hi⸗
ſtozies of olde ⸺
auncient anti⸗
quitie, and alſo
al godly ⸺ Chzi⸗
ſtiãwziters moſt
playnely conſẽt
together, and a⸗
gree in this, that dignitie, riches, kin⸗
red, wozdly pompe, and renoume, doo
neither make men better, ne yet hap⸗
piar, contrarie too the blynde ⸺ fonde
iudgement of the moſt part of menne:
but by the power and ſtrength of the
mynde, that is, learnyng, wyſedome,

A.ii.   and

and vertue, all menne are hyghly en=
riched, ornated, & most purely beuti=
fied,for these bee thinges bothe nota=
ble, eternall, and verye familiar be=
twene the heauenly father & vs . It
is therefore euidente (most excellent
Prince)that the fittest ornamētes for
your graces tender age, vec, cruditiō
and vertue. Wherunto you are bothe
so ernestly addicte and therin so wō=
derfully doo preuaile,that I nede not
too exhorte & exstimulate your grace
vnto the study thercof. For that God
him self hath wrought, and fourmed
your mynde so apt and desirous too
attayne and diligētly teo sceke for al
godly doctrine, that euē now you doo
shewe in all youre saipnges and doo=
inges suche a wonderfull pleasaūtes
much lyke vnto a certayne swete mu=
sike or harmonie,that any honest hart
exceadinglye woulde reioyce in the
sight thercof. Verely,your grace thin=
keth plainly all time lost , that is not
bestowed vpon learnyng , which is a
verie rare thyng in anye childe, and
rarest of all iu a Prince . Thus youre
noblenes, rather desireth vertue and
learnyng,

learning the most surest and excellent
treasures, which farre surmounte all
worldly ryches, then anye vanities or
trifles. Nowe youre grace prepareth
for the holsome and pleasaunt foode
of the mynde. Now you seke for that
whiche you shal fynd most surest hel=
per and faythfulst councellour in all
your affaires. Now your magnificēt
mynde studieth that, whiche all En=
glyshe menne with meke and humile
heartes shuld desire G O D to endue
your grace with all. Now with dili=
gent labour you searche for a thyng,
as one most myndeful of this saiyng:
Happy is that realme that hath a ler=
ned Prince. Nowe you trauaile for
that, whiche conquereth, and kepeth
doune all greuous tourmentes & out=
ragious affections of the mynde, too
the furderaunce of good liuyng, and
maintenaūce of vertue, I meane hol=
some erudition and learnyng. Many
Heathen Princes forsoth, are highly
magnified with most ample prayses,
which gaue them selues too the study
of Philosophie, or knowledge of ton=
gues, for their owne commoditie, and
    A.iii. especially

103

especially for the weale of their sub=
iectes. Who is nowe more celebrated
and worthelier extolled then Mithri=
dates? that noble kyng of Pont and
Bithinia, which, (as Aulus Gellius
writeth) vnderstoode so perfitly the
languages of.xxii. sondrye countries
that were vnder his dominō, that he
neuer vsed any interpretour too ans=
wer his subiectes, but spake their lā=
guages so finelye, as thoughe he had
been of the same coūtrie. Ageyn, that
honorable manne Quintus Ennius
said: that he had.iii. heartes, because
he coulde speake Greke, Italian, and
Latin. Yea, and breuely, the most fa=
mous writers, as well the Heathen,
as the Christien, with an vniuersall
consent, playnly affirme: Whan thei
had weied the nature and condiciō of
the purest thinges vnder heauen, thei
sawe nothyng faire, or of any pryce, or
that ought too be accōpted ours, but
onely vertue and learning. Euen now
too acknowledge that same, it is yeo=
uē you from aboue, for your grace de=
lecteth in nothyng more then too bee
occupied in the holye Byble: wherin,
                                              you

you beginne too sauer & smelle furth
the treasure of wisedome, knowledge
and fulnes of the deuyne power, that
is a studie most conuenient for euery
Christien Prince, that kynd of studye
cannot haue sufficient laude and com
mendation. Whose Princely heart
forsoth, is rauisshed on suche a godlie
and vertuous studie, it can neuer haue
condigne and worthie praises, but de=
serueth alwaies too bee had in great
price, estimation, and honour. Who
dooeth not know? that Prince which
is yeouen vnto the scriptures of God
and with a stoute stomake and valiāt
heart, both searcheth furth and also
defendeth ȳ true doctrine of the Gos=
pell, too bee inrolled in the assemble
of Christ. Who dooeth not see? that
Prince too bee moost surelye armed,
which carieth in his heart the swerd
of ȳ spirit, which is the blessed woord
of God. Who is ignoraunt? that euer
lastyng lyfe consisteth in the knowe=
ledge of God. What Prince woulde
not studie to maintaine that, which is
written for the health, and saluation
of all menne weyyuge with himselfe

A.iiii.   that

that a Prince can not deserue, neither
by conquest, ciuel policie, nor yet by a=
nye other meane vnder heauen, thys
name high or honorable, so wourthely
as by the setting forward of Goddes
woorde. What young Prince humily
descendyng doune intoo him selfe and
callyng to memory his bounden dutie
woulde not with a glad hearte and a
chearfull mynde, gredelye desyre too
knowe, enlarge, and amplifie the glo=
ry and maiestie of hys derely beloued
father? Your grace (forsoth) hath pro
fessed God too bee your father: Bles=
sed are you then if you obey vnto hys
word, and walke in his waies. Bles=
sed are you, yf you supporte suche as
preache the Gospell. Blessed are you,
yf your mind bee full furnished with
the testament of Christ, and shew your
selfe too bee the most cruel foo and e=
nemy agaynst ypocrisie, supersticion,
and all papistical phantasies, wherw
the true religion of God hathe been
dusked and defaced these many yeres
Blessed are you, if you reade it daye &
nighte, that your grace maye knowe
what GOD dooeth forbyd you, and
euer

euer submit your selfe therunto with
seruiceable lowlines chiefly desiring
to florysh and decke your mynd with
godly knowledge. And most blessed
are you,if you apply your self vnto al
good workes, & plant surely in your
heart the scriptures of Christ, If you
thus doo,nether the power of any pa=
pistical realme,nor yet of hel can pre=
uaile at any time against your grace.
Nowe therfore, with humile hearte,
faithfully receiue the swete promises
of the Gospel. If you kepe the woor=
des of the Lorde and cleaue fast vnto
them:there is promised you the king=
dome of heauen : You are promised a
weale publick most riche and welthy
You are promised too bee deliuered
from the deceiptes of all youre priuie
enemyes. You are promised also,too
conquere great and mightie nations.
Agayne,let your grace bee most fully
perswaded in this, that ther was ne=
uer Kyng nor Prince, that prospered
whiche tooke parte against Goddes
woord,and that the greatest abhomi=
nation that can bee, either for Kyng,
Prince,or any other manne,is too for
A.v.   sake

107

sake the true woord of God . O with
howe rebukefull woordes & greuous
iudgement thei be condemned, which
dispice & set lytle by the holy Byble &
most blessed Testamēt of God , wherin
there is containcd all the wil & plea=
sure of our heaūly father toward vs
most miscrable & ignorãunt wretches
Who would not quake , too beholde
the terrible feares & threatenynges
of God ageinst al suche? Who would
not lament & gladly helppe their ob=
stinate blyndenes ?   Who woulde
not weepe? to heare and reade iu how
many places, they be openly accursed
by the scriptures of Christ. God him
self playnely affirmeth, that he wyll
sodēly consume them with the breath
of his anger. Yea, besides that whoso
euer declyneth from the word of God
is accursed in all his doynges, whe=
ther he be Kyng , or Prynce , riche, or
poore, or of what estate soeuer he bee.
This fearfull sayng (most excellent
Prynce) shulde moue all men to take
hede vnto their duties and to prate
that gods word maie take place emō=
gist vs. O that al men would fanta=
sye

sie the scriptures of God, and saye w
the vertuous man Iob. Wee will not
bee ageynst the woordes of the holy
one. Truth it is, God taketh diligent
care too haue vs al know his woord.
Woulde God therfore, that all wee
were now willing to haue the syncere
woord of God & all holsom doctrine
too go forward. O that all we would
consent togither in the Gospell, bro=
therly admonishyng, and secretelye
prouokyng one an other too true reli=
gion & vertue. O that no man would
sow emongist the people pernitious
doctryne, but with all lowly diligéce
and Godlye monition euer prouoke,
tempt, and stere them, tyll their hear=
tes were remoued frô their olde dau=
tyng dreames and supersticiô, which
haue been long grafted in them tho=
row popyshe doctrine. By this meane
wee shuld euer haue concorde emon=
gist vs, whiche in all thynges is ne=
cessary, but most nedefull and expedi=
ent in Gods holi woord. Now truely
the godlyest thynge that can bee de=
uysed, for any christian realme, is to
haue emongist them one maner and
fourme

fourme of doctrpne,& too trace truell the steppes of God and neuer to seeke any other bpwapes.   Who hath not redde in þ scriptures?but that realme is endued with godlp oznamentes & riches, where all men pzospere,go foz ward and flozische in gods woozd, de= lectpng dap and night in the swete cō solations of the holp testament. By this wap we should especiallp setfozth the glozp of God,and of our sauiour Jesu Chzist, if we would reuerentlp shew one an other that whiche God hath taught vs. Yea & in this dopng all men shulde well perceaue that we were the true disciples of Chzist, be= ing knitte and coupled fast together in mpnde and iudgement, pzeachpng God with one mouth and also with one assent euer pzomotpng his glozp= ous testament.O the good happe and grace of that king oz pzpnce emongist whose subiectes there is such an hole consent and iudgement in the woozd of God, foz þ most assuredlp bpndeth & adiuigneth þ hartes of al subiectes too their kpng.   The strength of the Gospell is euen suche in this puincte, that

that there was neuer man, which did
humily receaue it, that would mur=
mour agaynst his Prince. It tea=
cheth how wyllyngly all men shulde
obey their kyng. It sheweth verye
lyuely and most apertly vnto euery
man his ful dutie. It euer prouoketh
vs from all wicked, cursed, and most
obstinate disobedience. It euer in=
structeth men too shewe them selues
most lowly, humile, and obesaunt to=
ward their Prynce. Whosoeuer hath
tasted fully therof, will declare hym
selfe in al thynges, too bee a faithful
subiect. Furthermore, it is clearer
then the light (most vertuous prince)
that it woulde make muche for the
weale of this noble realme, yf all mē
with heart and mynde, would nowe
as well expulse the pernitious and
deuelyshe doctryne of that Romishe
bishop, as his name is blotted ī boo=
kes. There is none so ignoraunt, but
he knoweth that thorough hym we
were brought into a wōderful blind=
nes, thorough hym we did sauer of
nothyng, but of stynkyng Ydolatry,
through hym we were deceiued with
false

false Ypocrisie. Now let euery blind
stiffe hearted,and obstinate creature
compare his abhomination with the
gospell,and if he be not shameles , he
will abasshe to smell of his papistrie,
and to walow still in ignoraunce,vn
lest he bee priuely confederate and in
heart consent with the detestable fe=
lowship of al wicked papistes. Now
would God all suche men would re=
duce ageyn their heartes vnto ẏ gos=
pell of Christ.would god they would
bee prouoked by some meane to de=
sire knowledge. O that god woulde
ȝeoue them a couragious mynde too
reade the gospel, there they shal sone
fynde all the venoume of the romishe
sort most playnely detected. Forsoth
wee see dayly,ẏ lacke of knowledge
of the gospel maketh some bussardes
runne hedlong on all rockes , daun=
gers,& extreme perilles: yea, and be=
side that,olde popysh doctryne whi=
che lyeth folded vp & locked faste in
their heartes,doeth so sore blynd thē
that they haue neither fauour ne af=
fectiō too printe in their myndes,the
expressed councels, admonitions , and
                                   preceptes

112

pꝛeceptes of the holy scriptnre, but
too slepe stil in their owne conceites,
dꝛeames,& fonde phansies. Wherfore
let your dignitie note well this,that
all those whiche bee not wyllyng ꝑ
gods wooꝛd should bee knowen, and
that blyndenes should be clean expul
sed from all men,whiche be baptised
in ꝑ blessed bludde of Chꝛist, bewꝛap
themselues playne papistes: foꝛ in
very deede that most deceatful wolfe
and graund maister papist with his
totiens quotiens,and a pena et culpa
blesseth all suche as will bee blynde
stil,maintaine his pōpe,dꝛinke of his
cuppe of foꝛnication,trust in his par=
dounes,liue in popery,ypocrisie,and
dānable ydolatrie, shut vp the king=
dome of heauen,& neuer regarde the
gospel. Cōtrarie too this,chꝛist bi his
holy Pꝛophete calleth al those bles=
sed ꝑ seke foꝛ his testimonies,al those
his elect & chosē childꝛē, which turne
frō synne,ypocrisie, & ydolatrie, all
those goddes ꝑ heare his woꝛd,yca,&
bꝛeuely,al those which set it foꝛward
honoꝛable mē.& in this puincte pour
grace shoulde euer beare in mynde,
that

that noble and vertuous kyng Heze=
kiah, whiche chewed hymſelfe very
honozable in ſettig fozward ÿ wooꝛd
of God, and therby gotte hym glozy
and fame immoꝛtall, ſo that nowe he
is moſt highly pꝛayſed emongiſt all
men. Ageyn his ſubiectes dyd obey
his commaundement feynedly with
Ypocriſie, but in their heartes they
abhoꝛred gods wooꝛd. O the miſerie
that dyd afterwarde ſodeinly enſue
vpon them, O the wonderfull wꝛath
of God that was poured vpon them,
O their great and obſtinate blindnes
whiche cauſed them moſt greuouſly
too be ſcourged: Their plage was no
leſſe then too bee vtterly ſpoyled of
their enemies, Their plage was no
leſſe then to eate one an other: Yea,
their plage was no leſſe then to eate
their owne ſonnes and doughters.
This calamitie and ſoꝛow (moſt no=
ble pꝛynce) happened them becauſe
they dyd not regarde the lawes of
God, but tourned too their olde ab=
hominable ydolatrie, and lightelye
eſtemed gods holy wooꝛd. Wherfoꝛe
euen now whoſoeuer is an enemie
tos

to the holy Bible, that is, neither stu=
dijng it himselfe, nor willyng that
other men shulde knowe it, he can in
no wyse be a right christian man: al=
though he fast, pray, doo almes, & all
the good workes vnder heauen. And
he that hath suche a mynde, is ŷ most
cursed and cruel enemie too god, a
playne sower of sedition, and a de=
uelishe disquieter of all godly men.
For truly those that reade the gospel
of Christ, and labour diligētly ther=
in: doo fynde wonderfull rest & qui=
etnes, from all woofull miserie, per=
turbatiō, and vanities of this world.
And surely none but ypocrites or els
deuilles would go about too stoppe
or allure men from suche a treasure
and godly study. And it were conue=
nient, that all they whiche wyll re=
mayne styll negligent, styffe, & blind
shuld set before their faces the feare
of paynes infernall, and if thei haue
any grace at all, their spirites ought
to be moued: too note the great pla=
ges that haue happened the slouth=
ful in gods woord, & those that haue
been stubburne ageynst the settyng

B.i.   out

115

out of it. There bee a thousand recordes and examples in the holy Bible agaynst such as be farre wyde from knowledge, and lye now walteryng styl in ignoraunce and will not looke vpon the bible. It wouloe seme, they hope for a thyng, but their hope is in vaine: For saint Paule plainely wrīteth the hope of suche ypocrites shall coom too noughr. And too conclude (most honorable Prince) seeyng wee haue suche knowledge opened vnto vs, as neuer had englishe mē, and are clearly deliuered from the snares and decceiptes of al false and wicked doctrine, if we shuld not now thākefully receaue the gospell, and shewe our selues naturally enclyned to set it forwarde, yea, and pray daye and night vnto God, for the preseruatiō and health of the kynges highnes, your graces deare, and most entierly beloued father, we were neither true subiectes nor ryght christen men. Forsoth, through the absolute wisedome, and the most godly and politike prudencie of his grace, the swete sounde of gods woorde is gone throrough

rough out all this realme, the holye
Bible and bleſſed teſtament of oure
ſauiour Chꝛiſt are coomne to lighte,
and thouſandes haue faithfully re=
ceiued thoſe pleaſaunt, ioyfull, and
moſt coomfoꝛtable pꝛomiſes of God.
Surely this thyng befoꝛe all other,
is acceptable too god. This thyng e=
ſpecially ſwageth ẏ ire of god.This
thyng in all holi ſcriptures god moſt
chiefly requireth of his elect ⁊ faith =
full ſeruaũtes, euen too haue his ly =
tell flocke knowe his bleſſed woo=
rde, whiche woulde bee muche better
knowẽ ⁊ moꝛe thankefulli receaued,
yf al ages and degrees of men with
one mynd, wyll, ⁊ voice, would nowe
Dꝛawe after one lyne, leauyng their
owne pꝛiuate affections, and ſhewe
theim ſelues euer vigilant, pꝛompt,⁊
ready helpers ⁊ woꝛkers with God,
(accoꝛdynge to the councell of ſainct
Paule)⁊ eſpecially pꝛieſtes, ſcolem aſ
ſters ⁊ parẽtes, which accoꝛdyng too
ẏ Pꝛophete Dauid are bleſſed, if they
gladly requite ẏ lawe of God. They
ſhuld therfoꝛe reade ẏ bible ⁊ puꝛdge
theyr mindes of al papiſtry: foꝛ theyꝛ

B.ii.   necli=

117

necligence,in dooyng their duties &
slugishnes toward þ blessed woord
of god,dooeth too muche appere.
Through them forsoth the gospel of
Christ shuld bee most strongely war=
ded and defended , for almost all the
Prophetes,and a great parte of the
scripture beside teache them their
duties,and shew playnely what ma=
ner of men they shulde bee: Yea, and
how greuously the holy Prophetes
crie out vpon false and ignorauut
priestes,the thyng is very euident.
But through the helppe of God all
those that be ignorauut, or els lear=
ned(as they take them selues) wyll
leaue of, and repent them of their
wicked and obstinate blyndnes,and
bowe them selues with all oportuni=
tie too draw mens heartes too the ho
ly testament of God: considerpng, þ
in the terrible day of iudgement , e=
uery mã shall proue accompte of his
Beliwicke,where neither ignorāce
shall excuse vs , ne yet any worldly
pōpe may defēd vs. Most happye thē
shall they bee, whiche haue walked
iustely in the sight of the Lorde , and
that

118

that haue syncerely preached his te=
stament and lyuely woord withoute
flattery or iuggelyng: Yea, and in ꝑ
fearful day, all they (as writeth) S.
Augustine) shal fynde mercie at the
handes of god, whiche haue entised
and allured other vnto goodnes and
vertue. Weiyng this with my self,
(most excellent, and vnto all kynd of
vertues most prompt & prestāt Prince)
I thought it good too translate this
Dialoge, called the Epicure, for your
grace : whiche semed too me, too bee
very familiar, & one of ꝑ godliest Di=
aloges ꝑ any mā hath writtē in ꝑ la=
tiu tong. Now therfore I most humi
lt praie, ꝑ this my rude & simple trās=
lation may bee acceptable vnto your
grace, trustyng also ꝑ your most ap=
proued gentilnes, wil take it in good
part. There as I doo not folow ꝑ la
tyn, woord for woord, for I omytte ꝑ
of a certaine set purpose.

Your humle seruaunt , Philyppe
Gerrard, groume of your
graces Chambre.
B.iii.

119

The inter=
locutours. { *HEDONIVS*

SPVDEVS.

HAT meaneth mt Spudeus, too applye hys booke so er= nestlye , I praye you what is the matter you murmour so with your selfe: SPVDEVS. The truth is (O Hedoni) I seke too haue knowledge of a thing, but as yet I cannot fynde þ whych maketh for my purpose. HEDO What booke haue you there in your bosome: SPVDE. Ciceros **dialoge**

dialoge of the endes of good=
nes. HEDO. It had bene farre
moze better foz you, too haue
fought foz the begynnynges of
godly thynges, then the endes.
SPVDE. Yea, but Marcus Tullius
nameth ꝫ the ende of godlines
which is an exquisite, a far paſ=
sing, and a bery abſolute good=
nes in euerye puincte, wherein
there is contained all kynde of
bertu: bnto the knowlcdge ther
of whoſoeuer can attaine, ſhuld
deſire none other thig, but hold
himſelfe hauyng onely that, as
one moſt fully content and ſa=
tiſfied. HED. That is a wozke
of bery great learning and elo=
quence. But doo you thynke, ꝫ
you haue pzeuailed in any thig
there, whereby you haue the ra=
ther

ther come too the knowledge of the truth: SPE. J haue had such fruite and cōmoditie by it, that now verelye hereafter J shall doubt moze of the effect and endes of good thinges, then J did befoze. HEDO. Jt is foz husbād menne too stande in doubt how farre the limittes and merchākes extend. SPE. And J can not but muse styll, yea, and wonder very muche, why ther hath been so great controuersie in iudgementes vpon so weightie a matter (as this is) emongist so well learned menne : especially suche as bee most famous and auncient wziters. HEDO. This was euen the cause, where the verite of a thyng is playne and manifest, cōtrarily, ÿ erroux thzough igno=

ignoɀaunce againe in the ſame,
is ſoone great ⁊ by diuers mea=
nes encreaſeth, foɀ ŷ thei knewe
not the foundation and firſt be=
ginnyng of the whole matter,
they doo iudge at all auentu=
res and are bery fondly diſcea=
ued,but whoſe ſentence thynke
you too bee trueſt?SPE. Whan
J heare MARCVS Tullius re=
pɀoue the thyng, J then fātaſſe
none of all their iudgementes,
and whan J heare hym agayne
defende the cauſe:it maketh me
moɀe doubtfull thē euer J was
and am in ſuche a ſtudie,that J
can ſay nothyng.But as J ſup
poſe ŷ Stoickes haue erred the
leſt, and nexte bnto thē J com=
mend the Peripatetickes. HEDo.
ret J lyke none of their opini=
ons

ons so well as I doo. the Epi=
cures. SPV. And emongist all the
sectes: the Epicures iudgement
is most reproued and condem=
ned with the whole consent and
arbitreinēt of all menne. HED.
Let vs laye a side all disdayne
and spite of names, and adinitte
the Epicure too bee suche one,
as euery man maketh of hym.
Let vs ponder and weighe the
thyng as it is in very deed. He
setteth the high and principall
felicitie of man in pleasure, and
thiketh that lyfe most pure and
godly, whiche may haue greate
delectatiō and pleasure, and ly=
tle pensiuenes. SPV. It is euen
so. HED. What more bertuon=
ser thyng, I praye you, is possi=
ble too bee spokē then this sai=
yng

saiyng. Spu. Yea, but all menne
wonder and crye out on it, and
saye: it is the voyce of a bruite
beast, and not of manne. Hedo.
I knowe thei doo so, but thei
erre in þ vocables of theise thin
ges, and are very ignozaunt of
the true and natiue significati-
ons of the woozdes, foz if wee
speake of perfecte thynges, no
kinde of menne bee moze righ=
ter Epicures, then Chzisten men
liuing reuerêtly towardes God
and mã, and in the right seruice
and wozshiping of Chzist. SPV
But I thinke the Fpicures bee
moze nerer and agree rather
with the Cynickes, then with the
Chzistien sozte: fozsoth þ Chzi=
stiens make them selues leane
with

with faftynge, bewayle and la=
ment their offences, and eyther
they bee nowe poo2e, o2 elles
they2 charitie and liberalitie on
the nedye maketh theim poo2e,
thei fuffer paciently too bec op=
p2effed of mène that haue great
power and take many w2onges
at their handes, and many men
alfo laughe theim too fko2ne.
Nowe, if pleafure b2ynge feli=
citie wyth it, o2 helpe in anye
wyfe vnto the furderaunce of
bertue: we fee playnly that this
kynde of lyfe is fardeft from al
pleafures . Hedonius. But doo
you not admitte Plautus too bee
of autho2itie? Speudeus. Yea, yf
he fpeake vprightely. Hedonius.
Heare nowe them, and beare a=
waye wyth you the faiynge of
an

an vnthziftie leruaunt, whyche
is moze wyttier then all the pa=
radoxes of the Stoickes .SPE.
I tarie to heare what ye wil lay
HEDO. Ther is nothyng moze
milerable then a mynd vnquiet
& agreued with it lelfe. SPE. I
like this laiyng well, but what
doo you gather of it? HEDO. If
nothing bce moze milerable thē
an vnquiet mynde, it foloweth
allo, that there is nothing hap=
piar, then a mynde voyde of all
feare, grudge, and vnquietnes
SPEV. Surely you gather the
thing together with good realō
but that notwithstandynge, in
what countrie shall you fynde
any luch mynde, that knoweth
not it lelfe gyltie and culpable
in some kynde of euell, HEDO.
I call

127

I call that euyll, whiche diſſol=
ueth the pure loue and amitie
betwirt God and manne. SPV.
And I ſuppoſe there bee verye
fewe, but that thei bee offēders
in this thynge. HEDO. And in
good ſoth I takc it, that al thoſe
ẏ bee purdged, are clere: whych
wiped out their fautes with lee
of teares, aud ſaltpeter of ſoꝛo=
wfull repentaunce, oꝛ els with
the fire of charitie, their offēces
nowe bee nɔt only ſmalle grefe
and vnquietnes too them, but
alſo chaunce oftē foꝛ ſome moꝛe
godlier purpoſe, as cauſing thē
too lyue afterward moꝛe accoꝛ=
dyngly vnto Gods commaũde=
mētes. SPV. In deede I knowe
ſaltpeter and lce, but yet I ne=
uer hearde befoꝛe, that faultes
haue

haue been purdged with fire.H?
Surely, if you go to the minte
you shall see gould fyned wyth
fyre, notwithstādyng that ther
is also,a certaine kynde of linē
that brenneth not if it bee cast
in ŷ fyre, but loketh more whi=
ter then any water coulde haue
made it, & therefore it is called
Linum asbestinum,a kynde of ly=
nen, whyche canne neither bee
quenched with water nor brent
with fyre .Spu. Nowe in good
faith you bring a paradox more
wōderful then all the maruai=
lous and profound thynges of
the Stoickes:lyue thei pleasa=
sauntly whom Chryst calleth
blessed for that they mourne &
lament ? Hedonius . Thei seme
too the worlde. too mourne, but
be=

129

verely they lyue in greate plea=
sure, and as the commune fai=
ynge is, thei lyue all together
in pleasure, in somuche that
SARDANAPALVS, Philoxe=
nus, oz Apicius compared vnto
them: oz anye other spoken of,
foz the greate desyze and study
of pleasures, did leade but a so=
rowefull and a myserable lyfe.
Spe. These thinges that you de=
clare bee so straunge and newe,
that I can scarcelye yeoue any
credite vnto them. Hedo. Pzoue
and assaye them ones, and you
shall fynde all my saiynges so
true as the Gospell, and immme=
diatly I shal bzyng the thynge
too suche a conclusion (as I sup
pose) that it shall appeare too
differ very lytle from the truth
Spe.

130

SPV.make hast then vnto your
purpose.HED. It shalbe doone
if you wyll graunt me certayne
thynges oʒ I begynne. Spu. If
in case you demaunde suche as
bee resonable.Hedo. I wyl take
myne aduauntage, if you con=
fesse the thyng that maketh foʒ
mine intent. Spu. go too. Hedo.
I thynke ye wyll fyʒste graunt
me,that ther is great diuersitie
betwꝛt the solle and the bodye
Spu. Euen as much as there is
betwene heauen and yearth,oʒ
a thyng earthly and bʒute , ꝓ ̄ỹ
whiche dieth neuer,but alway=
es cōtaineth in it the godly na=
ture. Hedo. And also, that false
decciueable ꝗ coū̄terfetted holy
thynges , are not too bee taken
foʒ those,which in very dede be
C.i   godly

godly. Spude. No more then the shaddowes are too bee estemed for the bodies, or the illusions and wonders of wytchcraftes or the fantasies of dreames, are too bee taken as true thynges. HE. Hitherto you answer aptly too my purpose, and I thynke you wyl graunt me this thyng also, that true and godly pleasure can reste and take place no where but only on such a mynd that is sobree and honest. SPV. What elles? for no man resoyseth too beholde the Sunne, if his eyes bee bleared or elles delecteth in wyne, if the agew haue infected hys tast. HED. And the Epicure hymselfe, or elles I am disceiued, would not clippe & enbrace that pleasure, whiche woulde

would bzing with it farre grea=
ter payne and suche as would
bee of long continuaunce.SPV
I thynke he woulde not, if he
had any wytte at all.HED.Noz
you wyll not denye this, that
God is the chiefe and especiall
goodnes,then whō there is no=
thyng fayrer, there is nothyng
ameabler,ther is nothing moze
delicious and swetter.SPVDE.
No man wyll deny thys except
he bee very harde hearted and
of an bngentlernature then the
Ciclopes.HED.Nowe you haue
graunted bnto me, that none
lyue in moze pleasure, then thei
whyche lyue bertuouslye ,and
agayne, none in moze sozowe
and calamytie then those that
C.ii.   lyue

lyue vngrattouſly.Spu.Then I
haue grauted moze the I thou=
ght I had.He.But what thing
you haue ones cofeſſed too bee
true(as Plato ſayth)you ſhould
not deny it afterward.SPV.Go
furth with your matter.HEDO
The litle whelpe ẙ is ſet ſtoze
and greate pzice by,is fed moſt
daintely, lieth ſoft,plaieth and
maketh paſtime continually,
doo you thinke that it lyueth
pleſautly?SPV.It dooeth true=
ly.HEDO. Woulde you wyſhe
to haue ſuche a lyfe? SPV. God
fozbyd that, excepte I woulde
rather bee a dogge then a man,
HEDO.Then you confeſſe that
all the chief pleaſures ariſe and
ſpzing frō the mynd,as though
it were from a welſpzyng.SPV.
That

That is euident ynough. HE. Fozsoth the strength and efficacy of the minde is so great, that often it taketh away the felyng of al externe and outward pain & maketh that pleasaunt, which by it selfe is very peynful. SPV. We se that dayly in louers, hauyng great delight to sytte vp long & too daunce attendaunce at their louers doozes all the colde wynter nyghtes. HEDo. Now weigh this also, if the naturall loue of man, haue suche great behemency in it, which is a cōmune thyng vnto vs, both with bulles and dogges, howe much moze should all heauenly loue excell in vs, which cōmeth of þ spirit of Chzist, whose strēgthe is of suche power, that it

C.iij   wold

would make death a thig most
terrible, too bee but a pleasure
vnto vs. Spu. What other men
thikc inwardly I knownot, but
certes thei wāt many pleasures
which cleaue fast vnto true and
perfect vertue. He. What plea=
sures? Spu. Thei waxe not rich,
thei optein no promotiō, thei bā
ket not, thei daūce not, thei sing
not, thei smell not of swete oynt
mētes, thei laugh not, thei play
not. He. We should haue made
no mention in thys place of ry=
ches and prefermente, for they
bryng wyth them no pleasaunt
lyfe, but rather a sadde and a
pēsiue. Let vs intreate of other
thynges, suche as they chiefely
seeke for, whose desyre is to liue
deliciously, see ye not daily dron=
ker=

kerdes, fooles, and mad menne
grinne and leaps? SPV. I sec it
HED. Do you thynke that thei
liue most pleasautly? SPV God
send myne enemies such myꝛth
& pleasure. HE. Why so? Sp. Foꝛ
ther lacketh emongist thē sobꝛi=
etie of mind. HE. Then you had
leuer sit fastyng at your booke,
then too make pastime after a=
ny suche soꝛte. SP. Of thē both:
truly I had rather chose to del=
ue. H. Foꝛ this is plaine that be
twixt the mad mā & the dꝛūkerd
ther is no diuersitie, but ꝑ slepe
wɩl helpe the one his madnes, &
with much a doo ꝑ cure of Phy=
sicions helpeth the other, but the
foole natural differeth nothing
frō a bꝛute beast except by shape
and poꝛtrature of body, yet thei
C.iiii   bce

be leſſe miſerable whom nature,
hathe made verye bʒutes , then
thoſe that walowe theim ſelues
in foule and beaſtly luſtes. SP.
I confeſſe that. Hedo.But now
tell me,whether you thynke thē
ſobʒe and wyſe,which foʒ playn
vanities and ſhadowes of ple‑
ſure, booth diſpice the true and
godlye pleaſures of the mynde
and choſe foʒ them ſelues ſuche
thynges as bee but veracion &
ſoʒowe.SPV. I take it, thei bee
not.Hedo. In deedethei bee not
dʒūke with wyne, but with loue
with anger,with auarice , with
ambicion, and other foule and
filthie deſires,whiche kynde of
dʒunkenes is farre woʒſe, thē
that is gotten with dʒinking of
wine. Yet Sirusꝗ̄ leude cōſpaniō
of

of whom mention is made in ý
commedie, spake witty thynges
after he had slepte hym self soo=
bȝe, and called too memoȝie
his greate and moost beastlye
dȝunkenes : but the minde that
is infected with vicious & nou=
ghty desire, hath muche a doo
too call it selfe whom agein?
How many yeares doeth loue,
anger, spite, sensualitie, excesse,
and ambition, trouble and pȝo=
uoke the mynde? How many
doo wee see, whiche euen from
their youth, too their latter dais
neuer awake noȝ repēt them of
the dȝunkennes, of ambitiō, ni=
gardnes, wanton lust, & riatte?
Spu. J haue knowen ouermany
of ý soȝte. Hedo. You haue graū=
ted that false and fayned good
thynges

thinges,are not too bee estemed
for the pure and godly. Sp. And
I affirme that still. Hedo. Nor
that there is no true and perfect
pleasure, except it bee taken of
honest and godly thynges.
Spud. I confesse that. He. Then
(I pray you)bee not those good
that the commune sorte seeke
for,they care not howe? Spu. I
thinke they be not.Hedo.Sure-
ly if thei were good,they would
not chaunce but onely too good
men: and would make all those
vertuous that they happen vn-
too.   What maner of pleasure
make you that , doo you thinke
it too bee godly,which is not of
true ⁊ honest thynges,but of de
ceatfull: and coometh out of ẏ
shadowes of good thynges? Sp.

Nay

Nay in noo wyse. He. For pleasure maketh vs to liue merely. Spu. Yea, nothyng so muche. He. Therfore no man truely liueth pleasauntly, but he that lyueth godly: that is, whiche vseth and delecteth onli in good thynges: for vertue of it selfe, maketh a man to habound in all thynges that bee good, perfcte, & prayse worthy: yea, it onely prouoketh God the fountaine of all goodnes, too loue and fauour man. SP. I almost consent with you. HED. But now marke howe far they bee from all pleasure, whiche seeme openly emongist all men too folowe nothyng, but an inordinate delectatiou in in thynges carnall.

First

141

First their mynde is bile, and
corrupted with the sauour and
taste of noughtie desires, in so
muche ꝑ if any pleasaunt thing
chaunce them, forthwith it war=
eth bitter, and is nought set by,
in like maner as where ꝑ welle
hed is corrupted and stynketh,
there ꝑ water must nedes be vn
sauery. Agein ther is no honest
pleasure, but that whiche wee
receaue with a sobre and a quiet
mynde. For wee see, nothyng re=
ioyseth the angry man more, thē
too bee reuenged on his offen=
ders, but that pleasure is tur=
ned into pain after his rage bee
past, and anger subdued. Spu.
J say not the contrary. He. Fi=
nally, suche leude pleasures bee
taken of fallible thinges, there=
fore

foze it foloweth that they be but delulios and shadowes. What woulde you say furthermoze, if you saw a mã so deceaued with sozcerie & allo other detestable witchecraftes,eat,dzynke, leap, laugh, yea, and clappe handes foz iove, when ther wer no such thyng there in very dede, as he beleueth he seeth. Spu. I wolde say he were both mad and mile= rable.Hedo. Jmy self haue been often in place, where the lyke thyng hath bcen doone. There was a pziest whiche knewe per= fectly by longe experience and pzactise, the arte to make thyn= ges seme that they were not, o= therwise called, deceptio visus, Sp.He did not lerne that arte of the holy scripture? Hedo.yea,ra ther

ther of most popeholy charmes
and witchecraftes : that is too
saye, of thinges, cursed, damp=
nable, and wourthy too bee ab=
hozred. Certayne ladies & gen=
tlewomen of the courte, spake
vnto hym oftentimes : saiyng,
they woulde coom one day too
his house and see what good
chere he kept:repzouyng, great=
ly vile and homly fare, and mo
derate expenses in all thynges.
He graunted they shulde bee
welcome, and very instauntly
desired them. And they came fa=
styng because they would haue
better appetites. Whã they wer
set to dyner(as it was thought)
ther wãted noo kynde of deliti=
ous meat : they filled thẽ selues
haboũdantly : after ỹ feast was
done

doone, they gaue moost hearty thanckes, for their galaunte cheare, and departed, euery one of them vnto their owne lod= gynges: but anone their sto= mackes beganne too waxe an hungred, they maruayled what this shuld meane, so soone to be an hungred and a thirste, after so sumptuous a feast: at the last the matter was openly knowen and laught at. Spu. Not with= out a cause, it had been muche better for thē too haue satisfied their stomackes at their owne chābers with a messe of potage, thē too be fed so delitiousli with bain illusiōs. H. And as I thiūk ẏ cōmune sort of men ar muche more too bee laught at, whiche in steede of Godlye thynges, chose

chose vaine and transitory sha=
dowes,and reioyce excedyngly
in suche folishe phansies that
turne not afterwarde in too a
a laughter,but into euerlasting
lamentation and sorow.Spudeus
The more nerelier I note your
saiynges,the better I like thē.
Hedo.Go too, let vs graunt for
a tyme these thynges too bee
called pleasaunt, that in very
dede ar not. Would yow saye
that meeth were swete : whiche
had more Aloes myngled with
it,then honye? Spud. I woulde
not so say and if there were but
the third part of an ounce of A=
loes mixt with it. Hedo. Orels,'
would you wishe to bee scabbed
because you haue some pleasure
too scratch? Spud.Noo,if I wer
iii

in my right mynd. HED. Then
weigh with your self how great
peyne is intermyngled wyth
these false and wrongly named
pleasures, ẙ vnshamefast loue
filthie desire, much eatyng and
drinking bring vs vnto: I doo
omitte now that, which is prin=
cipall grudge of cõscience, ene=
mitie betwixt God and mã, and
expectation of euerlastyng pu=
nishẽment. What kynd of plea
sure, I pray you is ther in these
thinges, that dooeth not bryng
with it a greate heape of oute=
ward euilles? SPV. What bee
thei? HEDO. We ought to let
passe and forbeare in this place
auarice, ambition, wrath, pryde
enuy, whiche of their selues bee
heuy and sorowful, euylles and
                              D.i   let

let vs conferre and compare all
those thynges together, ẏ haue
the name of some chief and spe=
cial pleasure:wher as the agew
the hedache ,the swelling of the
belly,dulnes of witte, infamy,
hurt of memory, vompting,de=
caye of stomacke, tremblyng of
the body succede of ouer muche
dzynking:thynke you, that the
Epicure would haue estemed a=
ny suche lyke pleasure as thys,
coucnient and wourthy desire:
SPV.He woulde saye it wer vt=
terly too bee refused.HEDONi.
Wheras young men also with
hauntynge of whozes (as it is
dayly seene) catche the newe le=
pzosie , nowe otherwyse named
Jobs agew,and some cal it the
scabbes of Naples , thzoughe
whiche

which deseafe they feele often ῷ
moſt extreme and cruell paines
of deathe euen in this lyfe, and
cary about abodye reſemblyng
very much ſome dead coarſe oʒ
carryn,do you thynke that theī
apply them ſelues vnto godlye
pleaſure.SPVD. Noo,foʒ after
theī haue been often familiar
with their pʒetyones, then they
muſt goo ſtreighte too the bar=
bours,that chaunceth continu=
allye vnto all whoʒemongers.
HED.Now fayne that ther wer
alyke meaſure of pain and ple=
ſure,would ye then require too
haue the toothache ſo longe as
the pleaſure of quaffing ⁊ whoʒ
dome endured ? SPV.Verely I
had rather wāt them booth, foʒ
ther is no commoditie noʒ van=
D.ii   tage

tage to bye pleaſure with payn
but only to chaũg one thing foʒ
another, but the beſt choiſe is
nowe not too affectionate anye
ſuch leudnes, foʒ MAR . Tullius
calleth that an inward greife ẜ
ſoʒow. He. But now ẏ pʒouoca-
tion ẜ entiſcmẽt of bnleful pleſure, beſides thatitis much leſſe
then the pain which it bʒingeth
with it, it is alſo a thing of a be
ry ſhoʒt time:but if the lepʒoſye
bee ones caught, it tourmẽteth
mẽ al their life daies bery piti-
fully ẜ oftentimes cõſtraineth
them to wyſhe foʒ death befoʒe
thei cã dye. SP. Such diſciples
as thoſe then, the Epicure would
not knowe. HED. foʒ the moſt
part pouertie, a bery miſerable
and painfull burden, foloweth
lechery

lechery, of immoderate lust cō= meth the palsie, tremblyng of ẏ senewes, blcardnes of eyes, and blyndnes, the lepzosie and not these only, is it not a pper pece of wozke(J pzay you) to chaũg this shozt pleasure neyther ho= nest noz yet godly, foz so manye euplles far moze grcuouse and of muche longer continuance. SP. Although there shoulde no pain com of it, J esteme hym to bee a very fond occupier, which would chaũge pzecious stones foz glasse. HE. you meane that would lose the godly pleasures of the mynde, foz the coloured pleasures of ẏ body. SP. That is my meanyng. HE. But nowe let vs come to a moze perfecter supputation, neither the agcwe

D.iii.   noz

noz yet pouerty foloweth alwai
es carnal pleasure, noz the new
lepzosy oz els the palsy waitnot
on at altunes the great & exces=
siue vse of lechcrye, but grudge
of cōsiēce euermoze is a folower
& sure companiō of al vnleaful
pleasure, then the which as it is
plainly agreed betwixt vs, no=
thyng is moze miserable. SPV.
Yea, rather it grudgeth their cō
science sometyme befoze hande,
& in the self pleasure it pzicketh
their mynde, yet ther bee some ÿ
you woulde say, want this mo=
tion and feelyng. HE. Thei bee
nowe therfoze in wozse estate &
cōditiō. Who would not rather
feele payne, then too haue hys
body lacke any perfecte sence,
truly from spme ether intempe=
ratnes

ratnes of euel deſires,euen like
as it were a certayne kynde of
dꝛunkenes,oꝛ els wont and cõ=
mune haunt of bice which ar ſo
hardened in them,ẏ they take a
way ẏ felyng ⁊ cõſideration of
euyl in their youth,ſo that whã
agee commeth bpõ them beſide
other infinitie hurtes and per=
turbations agaynſt whoſe com
myng thei ſhould haue layd bp
the deedes of their foꝛmer lyfe,
as a ſpecial iuwel and treaſure:
then thei ſtande greatly in fear
of death, a thyng emongiſt all
othermoſt ineuitable,⁊ that no
man canne ſhonne:pea, and the
moꝛe they haue heretofoꝛe been
dyſmayed and lackcd their ſen=
ces,the greater now is their bn
quietnes and grudge of conſ=

cience, then truely the mynde is
ſodenly awaked whether it wol
oz noo, and verely wher as olde
agee is alwayes ſad and heuy
of it ſelfe foz as muche as it is
in ſubiection and bondage vn=
to many incommodities of na=
ture, but then it is farre moze
wzetchede and alſo fylthye, if
the mynde vnquiet with it ſelfe
ſhal trouble it alſo: feaſtes, ryo=
tous banketyng, ſyngyng, and
daunſynge, with manye ſuche
other wanton topes & paſtimes
which he was communely ycō=
ué vnto & thought very pleſaút
when he was young, bee nowe
paynfull vnto hym beyng olde
and crooked, ne agee hath no=
thyng too comfozte and foztifi
hym

154

it selfe withall , but onely too
remembze that it hath paſſed o
uer the courſe of yeares in ber=
tue and godly liuyng and con=
ceaue a ſpecial truſt too obtaine
herafter a better kynde of life.
Theſe be the two ſtaues where=
bpon age is ſtayed,⁊ if in their
ſteed you wyll lay on hym theſe
two burdens: that is , memozie
how ſynfully he hath ledde his
life,and deſperation of the feli=
citie that is too coome, J pzaye
you what liuyng thyng can bee
feyned too ſuffre ſozer puniſhe=
ment and greater miſerie?. ſpu.
Uerely J can ſee nothyng al=
though ſome man woulde ſaye
an olde hozſe.hedo. Then to cõ=
clude it is too late to waxe wiſe
And that ſaiyng appereth now
too

too bee very true. Carefull moꝛ
nyngcs doo oftentymes folowe
mery euentides, and all vayne
and outragious mirth euer tur
neth into soꝛowfull sighes: yea,
& they shulde haue considered
both that there is noo pleasure
aboue ẏ ioyfulnes of the heart,
and that chearefull mynde ma=
keth agee too floꝛishe, an heauy
spirit consumeth the boones, &
also that all the dayes of the
pooꝛe are euell: that is, soꝛow=
full and wꝛetched. And agayne
a quiet mynde is lyke a conty=
nuall feaste. SPVDEVS. Ther=
foꝛe they bee wyse, that thꝛyue
in tyme, and gather too gether
nccessaries foꝛ that agee cooṁ.
HEDONI. The holy scrip=
ture intreateth not soo woꝛdely
as

as too meafure the felicitie and
highe confolation of manne, by
the goodes of fortune, onely he
is very poore, that is deftitute
and voyde of al grace & vertue,
and ftandeth in boundage and
debette, bothe of bodye & folle
vnto that tyranne oure mooft
foo & mortall enemie the deuill.
S.PV. Surely he is one that is
veri rigorous and impatient in
demaundynge of his dutie. HE.
Moreouer that man is ryche,
whiche fyndeth mercye and for=
yeouenes at the handes of god.
What fhuld he feare, that hath
fuche a protectour? Whether
men? where as playnely theyr
hole power may leffe do agaéft
God, then the bytyng of a gnat,
                              hurteth

hurteth the Elephant. Whether
death? truly that is a right paſ=
ſage foʒ good men vnto all ſuf=
ficient ioy and perfection accoʒ=
dyng too the iuſt reward of true
religion and vertue. Whether
hell? Foʒ as in that the holy pʒo
phete ſpeaketh boldely vnto
God. Although J ſhulde walke
in the middeſt of the ſhadow of
death, J wil not feare any euils
becauſe ÿ art with me. Wher=
foʒe ſhulde he ſtande in feare of
deuils , whiche beareth in his
heart hym , that maketh the de=
uils too tremble and quake.
Foʒ in diuers places the holye
ſcripture pʒaiſeth and declareth
opēly the mynde of a vertuous
man, too bee the right temple of
God. And this to bee ſo true ÿ
that

that it is not too bee ſpoken a=
gaynſt,nc in any wiſe ſhuld bee
denied.SPV. foꝛſoth I can'not
ſce,by what reaſon theſe ſaiyn=
ges of yours can be confuted al
thoughe they ſeine too barye
muche from the bulgar and cō=
mune opinion of men. HEDO.
Why doo they ſoo? SPV. After
your reaſonyng euery honeſt
pooꝛe man, ſhulde liue a moꝛe
pleaſaunt life, then any other,
how much ſoeuer he did haboūd
in riches,honour,and dignitie:
and bꝛeuely though he had all
kynde of pleaſuꝛes. HE. Adde
this too it (if it pleaſe you) too
bee a kyng,yea, oꝛ an emperour
if you take away a quiet mynd
with it ſelfe,I dare boldely ſay,
that the pooꝛe man ſklenderlye
and

and homely appareled, made
weake with faſtyng, watchyng,
great toile and labour, and that
hath ſcarcely a groat in all the
woꝛlde, ſo that his mynde bee
godly, he lyueth moꝛe deliciouſ=
ly then that man whiche hathe
fyue hūdꝛeth timesgreater plea
ſures & delicates, then euer had
Sardanapalus. SP. Why is it thē,
that we ſee communely thoſe
that bee pooꝛe lookc farre moꝛe
heuely then riche men. HED.
Becauſe ſome of them bee twiſe
pooꝛe, eyther ſome deſeaſe, ne =
dines, watchyng, labour, na=
kednesse, doo ſoo weaken the
ſtate of their bodyes, that by
reaſon therof, the chearefulnes
of their myndes neuer ſhew=
eth it ſelfe, neyther in theſe thin=
ges

160

ges, no; yet in their deathe. The
mynde, fo;footh thoughe it bee
inclofed within this mo;tal bo=
dye, yet fo; that it is of a ſtron=
ger nature, it ſõwhat trãſſour=
meth and faſcioneth the bodie
after it ſelfe, eſpecially if the ve
hement inſtigation of the ſpirit
app;oche the violent inclinati=
on of nature: this is the cauſe
we ſee oftentymes ſuche men
as bee vertuous die mo;e chere
fully, then thoſe that make pa=
ſtyme contynually, ⁊ bee yeoue
vnto al kynd of pleaſures. SP.
In very dede, I haue ineruay=
led oftten at that thyng. HED
Fo;foothe it is not a thyng too
bee inaruepled at, though that
there ſhulde bee vnſpeakeable
ioye

ioy and comforte where God is
is present, whiche is the heed of
all mirth and gladnes , nowe
this is no straunge thyng , al=
thoughe the mynde of a godly
man doo reioyce contynually in
this mortall bodye: where as if
the same mynde oʒ spirit discen=
ded into the lowest place of hell
shuld lose no parte of felicitie,
foʒ wherſoeuer is a pure mynd,
there is god, wher God is: there
is paradiſe, ther is heauen, ther
is felicitie, wher felicitie is: ther
is the true ioy and ſynſere glad=
nes. SP. But yet they shuld liue
moʒe pleaſauntly, if certein in=
conmodities were taken from
them, and had ſuche paſtymes
as eyther they diſpiſe oʒels can
not get noʒ attaine bnto. HE.

I

162

The Epicure

(I praye you) doo you meane,
suche incommodities as by the
commune course of nature fo=
low the condition or state of mã:
as hunger, thirst, desease, wery=
nes, age, death, lyghtnyng ye=
arthquake, fluddes & battail?
SPV. I meane other, and these
also. HEDO. Then we intreate
styll of mortal thynges and not
of immortal, & yet in these euils
the state of vertuous men, may
bee better borne withal, then of
suche as seeke for the pleasures
of the body they care not howe.
SPV. Why so: HEDO. Especy=
ally because their myndes bee
accustomed and hardened with
most sure and moderate gouer=
naunce of reason against al out
ragious affections of the mind

E.i.   and

The Epicure

(I praye you) doo you meane, suche incommodities as by the commune course of nature fo=low the condition or state of mã: as hunger, thirst, desease, wery=nes, age, death, lyghtnyng ye=arthquake, fluddes & battail? SPV. I meane other, and these also. HEDO. Then we intreate styll of mortal thynges and not of immortal, & yet in these euils the state of vertuous men, may bee better borne withal, then of suche as seeke for the pleasures of the body they care not howe. SPV. Why so: HEDO. Especy=ally because their myndes bee accustomed and hardened with most sure and moderate gouer=naunce of reason against al out ragious affections of the mind

E.i.   and

163

and they take moze patiently
thofe thynges that cannot bee
fhonned then the other fozt doo
Furthermoze, foz as muche as
thei perceiue, all fuch thynges.
ar fent of god, either foz the pu=
nifhment of their faultes, oz els
too excitate and fturre them vp
vnto vertue, then thei as mecke
and obediente chyldzen receiue
them from the hãd oftheir mer=
cifull father, not only defireou=
fly, but alfo chearefully and ge=
ue thankes alfo, namely foz fo
merciful punyfhment and ine=
ftimable gaines. SPV. But ma=
ny doo occatiõ griefes vnto thẽ
felues. HEDO. But mo feeke
remedye at the Phficions, either
to pzeferue theirbodies in helth
oz elles if they bee fycke, too re=
couer

couer health,but willyngly too
cause their owne sozowes, that
is,pouertie,sickenes,persecuti=
on,slaunder, exceptetheloue of
God compel vs therto,it is no=
vertue but folishnes:butas of=
often as thei bee punyshed foz
Chzist and iusticesake,who dar
bee so bold astoo cal them beg=
gers ⁊ wzetches? whā the Lozd
himself very famyliarly calleth
them blessed, and commaūdeth
vs to reiopse foz their state and
condition.SPV. Neuerthelesse,
these thynges haue a certayne
payne and griefe.HEDO.Thei
haue, but on the onesyde, what
foz fear of hel, and the other foz
hoope of euerlastynge iope, the
payne is sone past and fozgotte
Now tell me if you knewe that
E.ii.   you

you myghte neuer bee sycke, oz
elles that you shoulde feele no
payne of your body in your life
tyme , if you woulde but ones
suffer your vtter skinne too bee
przcked with a pynnes puinct,
would you not gladly and with
all your very heart suffer then
so lytle a payneas that is? SPV
Uerye gladlye, yea, rather if I
knewe perfectlye that my teeth
would neuer ake, I would wil-
lynglye suffer too bee przcked
depe with a nedle, and too haue
both mine eares bozed through
with a bodkin. HEDO. Surely
what payne soeuer happeneth
in this lyfe, it is lesse and shoz-
ter, compared with the eternall
paines, then is the soden pzicke
of a needle, incomparisõ of the
life

lyfe of man though it bee neuer
so long, for there is no conueni=
ence or proportion of the thyng
that hath ende, and that whych
is infinite. SPV. You speake be=
ry truly. HEDO. Now if a man
coulde fully perswade you, that
you should neuer feele payne in
al your life, if you did but ones
deuide the flame of ẙ fyre, with
your hande, whyche thyng vn=
doughtely Pithagoras forbade,
woulde you not gladlye doo it?
SPV. Yea, on that condicion I
had liefer doo it an hundred ti=
mes, if I knew precisely the pro
miser would kepe touch. HE. It
is playne God cannot deceaue.
But now that feelyng of paine
in the fyre is longer vnto the
whole lyfe of man, then is the

C.iii.   lyfe

lyfe of mã,in respect of the heauenlye ioye, althoughe it were thrise so long as ẙ yeares of Nestor,for that casting of the hand in the fyre thoughe it bee neuer so shorte,yet it is some parte of hys lyfe, but the whole lyfe of man is noo portion of tyme in respect of the eternal lyfe, SPV. J haue nothyng too saye against you.HEDO.Doo you then thyncke that anye affliction or tourment can disquiet thoie that prepare them selues wyth a chearful hearte and a stedfast hoope vnto the kyngedome of God,wher as the course of this lyfe is nowe so shorte? SPVDE. J thinke not,if thet haue a sure perswasion anda constant hope too attayne.it.HEDO.J coome nowe

now vnto those pleasures, whi=
che you obiected agaynst me,
they do wythdrawe them selues
from daunsynge, bankettynge,
from pleasaunte seeghtes, they
dispyce all these thynges , as
thus:for to haue the vse of thin
ges farre moze ioyfulle , and
haue as great pleasure as these
bee,but after another sozte : the
eye hath not seene,the eare hath
not heard,noz the heart of man
cannot thyncke what consola=
tions GOD hathe ozdeined foz
them that loue hym. Sayncte
Paule knewe what maner of
thynges shoulde bee the son=
ges,queeres, daunsynges, and
bankettes of vertuous myn=
des,yea,in this lyfe.SPVDEVS
but there bee some leafull plea=

sures, whyche they vtterlye re=
fuse. HEDONIVS. That maye
bee,foz the immoderate vse of
leafull and godly games oz pa=
stymes, is vnleaful: and if you
wyll exceptc this one thing on=
lye,in al other thei excelle whi=
che seems too leade a paynfull
lyfe,and whom we take too bee
ouerwhelmed with all kynd of
miscries. Now J pzai you what
moze roialler sight can ther be,
then y̆ cōtēplatiō of this wozld?
and such men as y̆ be in fauour
of god keping his holy cōmaū=
demētes & loue hismost blessed
testamēt,receiue far greater ple
asure in the syght therof,then
thother sozte doo, foz while thei
behold wyth ouercurious eyes,
y̆ wōderful wozke, their mynde
is

is troubled becaufe they can
not compaffe for what purpofe
he doeth fuch thinges, then thei
improue the mooft righte and
wife gouernour of all and mur=
mour at his doinges as though
they were goddes of reprehen=
fion: and often finde faute with
that lady nature, and faye that
fhe is vnnaturall, whiche taunt
forfooth with as muche fpite as
can bee fhewed with woordes,
greueth nature: but truely it re=
doundeth on hym, that made
nature, if there bee any at all.
But the vertuous man with
godly ᶜ fimple eyes beholdeth
with an excedyng reioyce of
heart the workes of his Lorde
and father highly praylyng thē
all, and neither reprehēdeth nor
fyndeth

171

findeth faut with any of thẽ, but
for euery thyng yeoueth moste
hearty thankes . when he confi=
dereth that al were made for the
loue of man . And so in all thyn=
ges, he praieth vnto the infinite
power, deuine wisedome, & good
nes of the maker, wherof he per=
ceiueth moste euident tokens in
thynges that bee here created.
Now fain that there were suche
a palace in verie deede as Apu=
leus faineth, or els one that were
more royall and gorgeousc, and
that you shoulde take twoo thi=
ther with you too beholde it, the
one a straunger, whiche gooeth
for this intent onely too see the
thyng, and the other the seruaũt
or soonne of hym that firste cau=
seth this buyldyng , whether
will

will haue moze delectie in it: the
straunger, too whom suche ma=
ner of house dooeth nothyng ap
partain, oz the soonne whiche
beholdeth with greate ioye and
pleasure, the witte, riches, and
magnificence of his deerely be=
loued father, especially when he
dooeth consider all this wozke
was made foz his sake. Sp. your
question is too plain: foz they
most comunely that bee of euill
condicions, knowe that heauen
and all thinges contained ther=
in, wer made foz mannes sake.
HEDO. Almoste al knowe that,
but some dooe not remembze it,
shewyng the selues bnthakeful
foz the great and exhuberat be=
nefittes of god, & al though thei
remember it, yet that ma taketh
greater

greater delight in the sight of it
whiche hath moze loue vnto the
maker therof,in like maner as,
he moze chearfully wyll behold
the element whiche aspireth to=
warde the eternall life. SPV.
Your saiynges are muche like
too bee true. HED. Nowe the
pleasures of feastes dooeth not
consist in the delicates of the
mouth, noz in the good sauces
of cookes,but in health of body
and appetite of stomacke. You
may not thynke that any delici=
ous person suppeth moze plea=
sauntly hauyng befoze hym par
triches,turtelles,leucrettes,be=
kers,sturgeon, and lampzayes:
then a vertuous man hauyng
nothig too eat,but onely bzead
potage,oz woztes;and nothyng
too

too dzynke, but water, single
bere, oz wyne well alayde, be
caule he taketh thele thinges as
pzepared of God vnto all ly=
uyng creatures, and that they
bee now yeoue vnto him of his
gentyll and mercifull father,
pzater maketh euery thyng too
fauour well. The petition in ỹ
begynnyng of dyner fanctificth
all thynges and in a while after
there is recited fome holy lefson
of the woozde of God: whiche
moze refrefheth the minde, then
meate the body, and grace after
all this. Finally he rifeth from
the table, not ful: but recreated,
not laden, but refrefhed: yea, re=
frefhed both in fpirit and bodie,
thynke you that any chief deui=
fer of thefe muche vfed bākets, ε
deyntie

deintye delicaces fareth nowe
moze delicioufly? SPudeus. But
in Venus there is greate delecta=
cions if we beleue Areftotell.Hed.
And in this behalfe the vertu=
ous manne far excelleth as well
as in good fare,wiegh you now
the matter as it is, the better a
manne loueth his wife,the moze
he delecteth in the good felow
fhip and familiaritie that is be=
twene them after the courfe of
nature.Furthermoze, no menne
loue their wiues moze veheme=
tly then thei that loue them eue
foo,as Chzift loued the churche.
Foz thei that loue the foz the de=
fire of bodely pleafure, loue the
not.Moze ouer, the feldomer a=
ny man dooeth accompany with
his wife, the greater pleafure,it
is

is to hym afterwarde, and that
thyng the wāto poete knew full
well whiche wziteth, rare and sel
dome vse stereth vp pleasures.
Albeit, the lest parte of pleasure
is in the familiare company betwene theim. There is fozsothe
far greater in the continuall lea
dyng of their liues too gether,
whiche emongest none can be so
plesaunt as those that loue syn=
cerely and faithfully together
in godly and chzistian loue, and
loue a like one the other. In the
other sozt, ofte whē the pleasure
of ẏ body decaieth & waxeth old
loue waxeth coold & is sone foz-
gottō, but emōgest right chzistē
mē, the moze ẏ the lust of ẏ flesh
decreaseth & banishethaway, ẏ
moze thē al godly loue encreseth
                              Are

177

Are you not yet perſwaded that none lyue moꝛe pleaſauntly thē they whiche liue continually in vertue and true religiō of god? SP. Would god all men were as well perſwaded in that thyng. He. And if they bee Epicures ꝙ lyue pleaſauntli:none bee righ ter Epicures then they that liue vertuouſly,and if we wyll that euery thyng haue it right name none deſerueth moꝛe ꝙ cogname of an Epicure,then that Pꝛince of all godly wiſedome too whō moſt reuerētly we ought alwai es too pꝛaye : foꝛ in the greeke tonge an Epicure ſignifieth an helper. Nowe whan the lawe of nature was firſt coꝛrupted with ſinne,whē the law of Moſes dɩd rather pꝛouoke euil deſires thē reɩne

then remedy them.Whã the ty=
raunte Sathanas reygned in
this worlde freely and wythout
puniſhement,then thys prynce
onely, dyd ſodenlye helpe man=
kynde redy to periſhe:wherfore
thei erre ſhamefully which ſcoff
and bable that C H R I S T was
 one that was ſadd and of a ma=
lancolye nature , & that he hath
prouoked vs vnto an vnplea=
ſaunt kynde of lyfe,for onely he
did ſhewe a kind of liuing moſt
godly andfulleſt of al true plea
ſure,if we might haue the ſtone
of Tantalus taken awaye from
vs.SPVD.What darke ſaiyng
is this? EDO. Jt is a mery tale
too laugh at, but this bourd in
duceth verye graue and ſadde
thynges.SPV.J tary too heare
f.i. this

this mery conceite, that you na=
me too bee so sage a matter. HE
¶Thei whiche gaue their studye
and diligence to colour and set=
furth the preceptes of Philoso=
phie wyth subtil fables, declare
ÿ there was one Tantalus brou=
ghte vnto the table of the god=
des, whych was euer furnished
wyth all good fare, and most
nete and sumptuous that my=
ght bee, whan thys straunger
shoulde take hys leaue, Jupy=
ter thought it was for his great
liberalitie and highe renoume,
that his guest shuld not depart
wythout some rewarde, he wyl=
led him therfore too aske what
he woulde, and he shoulde haue
it: Tantalus (forsooth) lyke a ve=
rye leude and foolyshe person,
for

180

foz that he sette all the felicitie
and pleasure of man in the de=
lectation of the bely,and gloto=
nye, desired but only too sytte
at suche a table all the dayes of
hys life, Iupiter graunted him
his desire, and shoztly his vow
was there stablished and ratt=
fyed. Tantalus nowe sytteth at
the table furnyshed wyth all
kindes of delicates,such dzinke
as the goddes dzuncke of was
set on the table, and there wan=
ted no rooses noz odours that
could yeouc any swete smel be=
foze the Goddes, Ganymedes the
buttler oz one lyke vnto hym,
standeth euer redye, the Muses
stande rounde aboute syngyng
pleasauntly,inery Silenus daun=
seth,ne ,ther wanted noo fooles

F.ii.   too

too laugh at,and bȝeuely,there
there was euerye thynge that
coulde delyght any sence of mã
but emongiſt all theſe, Tantalus
ſytteth all ſadde, ſyghyng, and
vnquiet with hym ſelfe,neither
laughing noȝ yet touching ſuch
thynges as were ſet befoȝe hym
SPVDE. Ƿhat was the cauſe᷅
HED. Ouer his head as he ſate
there hãged by an hecre a great
ſtone euer lyke too fall. S PV.Ꝑ
woulde then haue conueied my
ſelfe from ſuche a table. HEDÓ
But his vowe had bound hym
too the centrarye, foȝ Ꝺuppter
is not ſo eaſye too intreate as
oure GOD, which dooeth vn=
looſe the pernitious bowes of
mehne,that bee made contrary
vnto his holy wooȝd,if thei bee
pent=

penitent and ſoꝛye therfoꝛe, oꝛ
elles it myght bee thus, the ſa=
me ſtoone that woulde not ſuf=
fer hym too eate, would neither
ſuffer hym to ryſe, foꝛ if he had
but ones moued he ſhuld haue
been quaſhed al in peeſes with
the fall thereof. SPVDE. You
haue ſhewed a very mery fable
HEDON. But nowe heare that
thing, which you wil not laugh
at: the commune people ſeeke
too haue a pleaſaunt life in out
warde thynges, where as noo=
thyng can peoue that, but one=
ly a conſtant and a quiet mind:
foꝛ ſurely a far heuier ſtone han
geth ouer theſe ẙ grudge with
them ſelues, then hanged ouer
Tantalus: it only hangeth not
ouer them, but greueth and op=
F.iii. pꝛeſſeth

preſſeth the mynde,ne the mind
is not troubled wyth any vayn
hoope,but looketh euery houre
to bee caſte in too the paynes of
hell, I praye you what can bee
ſo pleaſaunt emongiſt all thin=
ges that bee yeouen vnto man,
that coulde reioyſe the mynde,
whyche were oppreſſed wyth
ſuche a ſtoone:SPVDE.Cruely
there is nothyng but madnes,
or elles incredulitie.HEDO. Yf
younge menne woulde weygh
theſe thynges,that bee quyckly
prouoked and entiſed with plea
ſure as it were wyth the cuppe
of Circes, whiche in ſteade of
theyr greateſt pleaſures recei=
ue poyſone myxte wyth honye.
Howe circumſpecte would they
bee-too doo anye thynge vnad=
uiſedly

uisedly ȳ shoulde grudge their
mindes afterward? What thin
ge is it that thei would not doo
too haue suche a godly treasure
in stoꝛe against their latter dai=
es?that is a minde knowyng it
selfe cleane ⁊ honest and a name
that hath not been defiled at a=
ny time. But what thyng now
is moꝛe miserable then is agee?
Whan it beholdeth,and loketh
backward on thinges ȳ be past
seeth plainly with great grudg
of conscience howe fayꝛe thyn=
ges he hathe despiced and sette
lyght by,(that is,howe farre he
hath discented and gone astray
from the pꝛomyses made vnto
God in baptime) ⁊ agayn, how
foule ⁊ noughty thiges he hath
clipped and enbꝛaced,and whā

F.iiii   be

hee looketh fozwarde, hee seeth
then the daye of iudgemente
dzawe neere, and shoztely after
the eternall punyshemente of
of hell. SPVDE. I esteme theim
most happie whych haue neuer
defyled theyz youthe, but euer
haue increased in bertu, til thei
haue coomne bnto the last pu=
incte of age. HEDO. Next them
thei ar too bee commended that
haue wythdzawne theim selues
from the folie of youth in tyme.
SPVDE. But what councel wil
you peoue agee that is in suche
great myserie. HEDO. No man
shoulde dispayze so long as life
endureth, I wyl exhozte him to
flee foz helpe bnto the infinitie
mercye & gentilnes of God. SP.
But the longer § he hath liued
the

the heape of his synnes hath e=
uer waxen greate and greater,
so that nowe it passeth the nom=
ber of the sandes in the sea, HE
But the mercies of our lord far
excede those sādes, for although
the sande can not bee numbred
of manne, yet hit hath an ende,
but the mercie of God neither
knoweth ende, ne measure. SP.
yea but he hath no space that
shall dye by and by, HEDONI.
The lesse tyme he hath the more
feruētly he should cal vnto god
for grace, that thyng is long
inough before God, whiche is
of suche power as too ascende
from the yearth vnto heauē, for
a short prayer forsoth streght en
treth heauē, if it bee made with
a behemēt spirit. It is written, ȳ
the

ẏ womã synner spoken of in the
gospell did penaunce al her life
dayes: but with how fewe wo2=
des again did the thief obtain
Paradise in the houre of death?
If he will crye with hearte and
mynde, God haue mercie on me
after thy great mercie: God wil
take awaye from hym Tantalus
stone and yeoue in his hea=
ryng ioye and cõfo2t
and his bones hu=
miled th2oughe
cõtrition, wil
reioyse
that
he
hath his synnes
fo2 yeouen
hym.
FINIS.

188

Imprinted at London vvithin the
precinct of the late diſſolued houſe
of the gray Friers, by Richarde
Grafton, Printer too the
Princes grace.
the. X X I X.
daie of Iuly, the yere
of our Lorde.
M. D. X L V.

191

❡ Two dyaloges wrytten in laten

by the famous clerke. D. Eras-
mᵘˢ of Roterodame/ one called
Polyphemus or the gospeller/
the other dysposyng of thynges
and names/ translated
in to Englyshe by
Edmonde
Becke.
And prynted at Cantorbury
in saynt Paules parysshe
by John Mychell.
✠

Lucius Anneus Seneca amonge many other pratie satenges (gentle reder) hathe this also, whiche in my iudgement is as trew as it is wittie. Rogādo cogit qui rogat superioz. And in effecte is thus moch to say, yf a mānes superioz oz his better desyze any thige, he might alwell cōmāde it by authozitie as ones to desyze it. A gentleman a nere colyn of myne, but moch nerer in fryndshyp, eftesones dyd instant and moue me to translate these two dyaloges folowynge, to whose getlenes I am so moch obliged, indetted and bounde, that he myght well haue cōmaunded me to this and moze paynes: to whome I do not onely owe seruyce, but my selfe also. And in accōplyshynge of his most honest request (partly bycause I wolde not the moost inhumane fawte of Ingratitude shuld

A.ii.

195

chely be imputed to me, & that I might
in this thynge also (accozdynge to my
bounden dutie) gratifie my frende) I
haue hassard my selfe in these daunge=
rous dayes, where many are so capcy=
ous, some pzone and redy to malygne &
depzaue, and fewe whose eares are not
so festidious, tendze, and redy to pleese,
that in very tryfles & thynges of small
impoztaunce, yet exacte dylygence and
exquisite iudgement is loked foz and re=
quyzed, of them whiche at this pzesent
wyll attempte to translate any boke be
it that the matter be neuer so base. But
what diligence I haue enployed in the
translactō hercof I referre it to the iud
gement of the lerned soz, whiche cōfer
rynge my translacion with the laten dy
aloges, I dowte not wyl condone and
pardone my boldnesse, in that that I
chalenge the semblable lybertie whiche
the translatours of this tyme iustlie
chalenge. Foz some here tofoze submyt
tyng them selfe to seruptude, haue lytle
respect

196

respecte to the obseruacyõ of the thyng
which in translacyõ is of all other moste
necessary and requisite, that is to saye,
to rendre the sence & the very meanyng
of the author, not so relygyouslie ad=
dicte to translate worde for worde, for
so the sence of the author is oftentimes
corrupted & depraued, and neyther the
grace of the one tonge nor yet of the o=
ther is truely obserued or aptlie expres=
sed. The lerned knoweth ȳ euery tonge
hathe his peculyer propriette, phrase,
maner of locucion, enargies and vehe=
mécie, which so aptlie in any other tõg
can not be expressed. Yf I shal perceyue
this my symple doinge to be thankeful
ly taken, and in good parte accepted, it
shall encorage me hereafter to attempte
the translaciõ of some bokes dysposing
of matters bothe delectable, frutefull, &
expedient to be knowen, by the grace of
God, who gyuynge me quyetnes of
mynde, lybertie, and abylytie, shall not
delyste to communicat the frute of my
                                    spare

spare howers, to such as are not lerned in the laten tonge: to whome I dedycat the fyrste srutes of this my symple translacyon.

A declaracion of the names.

POliphemus sygnifieth, valyant or noble, and in an other sygnifi cacion, talcatyse or clybbe of tong. The name of a Gyant called Cyclops, hauynge but one eye in his forhed, of a huge stature and a myghtie psonage. And is aplyed here to sygnifie a great freke or a lubber, as this Poliphemus was, whiche beynge a man of warre or a courtyer, had a newe testament in his hande, and loked buselie for some sentence or text of scrypture and that Cannius his companyo̅ espyed and sayd to hi as so= loweth.

The

198

¶ The parsons names are
Cannius and Poliphemus.

Annius. what hunt Poliphe=
me for here? Poliphem⁹. Aske
ye what I hunt for here, and
yet ye se me haue neyther dogges, dart,
Iauelyn, nor huntyng staffe. Cannius.
Paraduenture ye hunt after some pra=
ty nymphe of the couert. Poliphemus.
By my trouth and well contectured, be
holde what a goodly purlenet, or a bay
I haue here in my hande. Canni⁹. Be=
nedicite, what a straunge syght is this,
me thinke I se Bachus in a lyons skin,
Poliphemus with a boke in his hande.
This is a dogge in a doblet, a sowe w
a sadle, of all that euer I se it is a non
decet. Poliphe. I haue not onely payn=
ted and garnyshed my boke with saf=
fron, but also I haue lymmed it withe
Sinople, asaphetida, redleed, vermilō,
and byse. Can. It is a warlyke boke,
for it is furnished with knottes, tassils
plates,

199

plates, clalpes, and brasen bullyons.
Poliphe. Take the boke in your hand
and loke within it. Canni. J le it wery
well. Truly it is a praty boke, but me
thynkes ye haue not yet trymmed it
sufficiently for all your cost ye haue be=
stowed vpon it. Poliphe. why what lae
kes it? Cannt. Thou chuldest haue set
thyne armes vpon it. Poliphem9. what
armes J beleche the? Cāni9. Mary the
heed of Silenus, an olde iolthed drun=
kard totynge out of a hoggeshed or a
tunne, but in good erneft, wherof dothe
your boke dyspose or intreate? dothe it
teache the art and crafte to drynke a
duetaunt? Polt. Take hede in goddes
name what ye lay left ye bolt out a blal
phemie before ye be ware. Cāni9. why
bydde ye me take hede what J laye? is
there any holy matt in the boke? Polt.
what mā it is the golpell boke, J trow
there is nothynge can be more holye.
Canni9. God for thy grace what hathe
Poliphemus to do withe the golpell?
Polt.

Polt. Nay why do ye not aske what a chꝛyſten man hathe to do with chꝛiſte-Cannt⁹. I can not tell but me thynkes a rouſty byll oꝛ a halbard wold become ſuch a great lubber oꝛ a ſlouyn as thou arte a great deale better, foꝛ yf it were my chaúce to mete ſuch one and knewe him not vpon ſeeboꝛde, and he loked ſo lyke a knaue and a ruffyã as thou doſt I wolde take hym foꝛ a pirate oꝛ a ro-uer vpon the ſee/ and if I met ſuch one in the wood foꝛ an arrante theſe, and a man murderer. Polt. yea good ſyꝛ but the goſpell teache vs this ſame leſſon, that we ſhuld not iudge any perſon by his loke oꝛ by his externall & outwarde apparaunce. Foꝛ lyke wyſe as many tymes bnder a graye freers coote a ty-rannous mynde lyeth ſecretly hyd, eue ſo apolled heed, a criſpe oꝛ a twyꝛled berde, a frowninge, a ferſe, oꝛ a dogged loke, a cappe, oꝛ a hat with an oyſtrich fether, a ſoldyers caſſocke, a payꝛe of hooſe all to cut and manglyd, may co=
uer

net an euangelycall mynde. Cannius.
why not, mary God forbyd elles, yea a
many tymes a symple shepe lyeth hyd
in a wolfes skynne, and yf a man maye
credite and beleue the fables of Aesope,
an asse maye lye secretely vnknowen by
cause he is in a lyons skynne. Poliphe.
Naye I knowe hym whiche bereth a
shepe vpon his heed, and a fore in his
brest, to whome I wold wysshe with al
my hart that he had as whyte and as
fauorable frendes as he hathe blacke
eyes. And I wolde wysshe also that he
were aswell guylt ouer and ouer as he
hathe a colour mete to take guyltynge.
Cannt. Yf ye take hym to were a shepe
vpon his heed, that weareth a cappe of
woll, howe greuously than art thou lo
dyn, or what an excedynge heuy burde
bearest thou then I praye the whiche
bearest a hoole shepe and an ostryche to
vpon thy heed? But what saye ye to hi
doth not he more folysslye whiche beareth
a byrd vpon his heed, and an asse in his
brest.

202

bꝛest.Poliphemus.There ye nypped & taunted me in dede. Cannius. But I wolde saye this geere dyd wonderous wel yf this gospel boke dyd so adourne the with vertue as thou hast adourned lymmed, and goꝛgiously garnysshed it with many gay goodly glystryng oꝛnamentes.Mary syꝛ thou hast set it foꝛth in his ryght colours in dede, wolde to god it might so adourne the with good códiciós that thou myghtest ones lerne to be an honest man.Poli. There shall be no defaute in me, I tell you I wyll do my diligence.Can.Naye there is no doute of that, there shall be no moꝛe faute in you now I dare say then was wonte to be.Poli.Yea but(youre tarte tauntes,and youre churlysshe checkes, and raylynges set asyde)tell me I pꝛay the this one thynge, do you thus dispꝛayse,condempne, oꝛ fynde faute with them whiche caryeth aboute with them the newe testament oꝛ the gospel boke? Canni.No by my fayth do I not good pꝛay

praty man. Poliphe. Call ye me but a
praty one and I am hygher then you
by ye length of a good asses heed. Can.
I thynke not fully so moche yf the asse
stretch forth his eares, but go to it skyl
lis no matter of that, let it passe, he that
bare Christ vpon his backe was called
Christofer, and thou whiche bearest the
gospell boke aboute with the shall for
Poliphemus be called the gospeller or
the gospell bearer. Polip. Do not you
counte it an holy thynge to cary aboute
with a man the newe testament? Cani.
why no syr by my trouth do I not, ex=
cept thou graunte the very asses to be
holy to. Poli. How can an asse be holy?
Cannius. For one asse alone is able to
beare thre hundreth suche bokes, and
I thynke suche a great lubber as thou
art were stronge inoughe to beare as
great a burden, and yf thou had a han=
some packesadle sette vpon thy backe.
Poliphe. And yet for all your iestynge
it is not agaynst good reason to saye
that

that ŷ asse was holy whiche bore chriſt.
Cannius. I do not enuye you man for
this holynes for I had as lefe you had
that holynes as I, and yf it pleaſe you
to take it I wyll geue you an holy & a
religious relyke of the ſelfe ſame aſſe
whiche chriſt rode vpon, and whan ye
haue it ye may kyſſe it lycke it and cull
it as ofte as ye lyſt. Poli. Mary ſyr I
thanke you, ye can not gyue me a more
thanckefull gyfte nor do me a greatter
pleaſure, for that aſſe withouten any
fayle was made as holye as any aſſe
could be by the touchynge of chriſtes
body. Canni⁹. Undouted they touched
chriſtes body alſo whiche ſtroke and
buffeted chriſt. Poliphe. yea but tell me
this one thynge I praye the in good
erneſt. Is it not a great ſygne of holynes in a man to cary aboute the goſpel
boke or the newe teſtament? Cannius.
It is a token of holynes in dede if it be
done without hypocryſie, I meane if it
be done without diſſimulacion/and for
                                        that

205

that end, intent & purpose, that it shulo be done for. Poliphe. What the deuyl & a morren tellest thou a man of warre of hypocrisie, away with hypocrisie to the monkes and the freers. Cannius. Yea but bycause ye saye so, tell me fyrste I praye you what ye call hypocrisie. Po. When a man pretendis another thyng outwardly then he meanis secretly in his mynde. Cannius. But what dothe the bearynge aboute of the newe testament sygnyfie. Dothe it not betoken that thy lyfe shulde be conformable to the gospell which thou carryest aboute with the. Polt. I thynke well it dothe. Canni⁹. wel then when thy lyfe is not conformable to the boke, is not that playne hypocrisie. Poliph. Tell me the what you call the trewe carienge of the gospell boke aboute with a man. Cant. Some men beare it aboute with them in theyr hades (as the gray freers were wonte to beare the rule of sayut Fraunces) and so the porters of Londō, Asses and

& hoɼſes may beare it as well as they. And there be ſome other that carry the goſpel in theyɼ mouthes onlie, and ſuch haue no other talke but al of chɼiſt and his goſpell, and that is a very poynt of a pharyſey. And ſome other carrye it in theyɼ myndes. But in myne opynion he beares the goſpell boke as he ſhuld do whiche bothe beares it in his hande, cõ munes of it with his mouth whan occa ſyon of edyfyenge of his neyghboure whan conuenyent opoɼtunytie is my nyſtred to him, and alſo beares it in his mynde and thynkes vpon it withe his harte. Poli. Yea thou art a mery felow, where ſhall a man fynde ſuche blacke ſwãnes? Cannius. In euery cathedɼall church, where there be any deacons, foɼ they beare the goſpel boke i theyɼ hãde, they ſynge the goſpell aloude, ſomtyme in a lofte that the people may heare thẽ, althoughe they do not vnderſtand it, and theyɼ myndes are vpõ it when they ſynge it. Polphe. And yet foɼ all your

ſayenge

sayenge all suche deacons are no saync=
tes that beare the gospell so in theyz
myndes. Cannius. But lest ye play the
subtyle and capcious sophystryar with
me J wyll tell you this one thynge be=
foze. No man can beare the gospell in
his mynde but he must nedes loue it
from the bothum of his harte, no man
loueth it inwardly and from the bothū
of his harte but he must nedes declare
and expresse the gospell in his lyuinge,
outwarde maners, ꝛ behauour. Poll.
J can not skyll of youre subtyle reaso=
nynges, ye are to fyne foz me. Can. Thē
J wyll commune with you after a grof
fer maner, and moze playnly. yf thou
dyddest beare a tankard of good Rey=
nysche wyne vpon thy shulders onelye,
what other thynge were it to the then a
burden. Poliphe. Jt were none other
thynge truly, it is no great pleasure to
beare wyne. Cannt⁹. What and yf thou
dranke almoche as thou coudest well
holde in thy mouthe, after the maner of
a gargarisme

a gargarísme ⁊ ſpyt it out agayne. Po. That wolde do me no good at all, but take me not with ſuche a faute I trow, foꝛ the wyne is very bad and if I do ſo. Canni. But what and yf thou dꝛynke thy ſkynne full as thou art wont to do, whē thou comeſt where good wyne is. Poliphe. Mary there is nothyng moꝛe godly oꝛ heuynly. Canni⁹. It warmes you at the ſtomacke, it ſettes your body in a heate, it makes you loke with a ruddy face, and ſetteth your hart vpon a mery pynne. Poliphe. That is ſuerly ſo as ye ſaye in dede. Canni. The goſpell is ſuche a lyke thynge of all this woꝛlde, foꝛ after that it hathe ones per=ſed ⁊ entered in the veynes of the mynd it altereth, tranſpoſeth, and cleane chan geth vpſodowne the whole ſtate of mā, and chaungeth hym cleane as it were into a nother man. Polip. Ah ha, nowe I wot wherabout ye be, belyke ye thike that I lyue not accoꝛdynge to the goſ=pell oꝛ as a good goſpeller ſhulde do.

B.i.   Canni.

Canni⁹. There is no man can dyſſolue this queſtiõ better then thy ſelfe. Poli. Call ye it diſſoluynge: Naye and yf a thynge come to dyſſoluynge gyue me a good ſharpe axe in my hande and I trow I ſhall dyſſolue it well inoughe. Canni. what woldeſt thou do, I praye the, and yf a man ſhulde ſay to thy teth thou lyeſt falſely, oz elles call the by thy ryght name knaue in englyſche. Poli. what wolde I do quod he, that is a queſtion in dede, mary he ſhulde feele the wayghte of a payze of churlyſche fyſtes I warrant the. Canni. And what and yf a man gaue you a good cuffe vp= on the eare that ſhulde waye a pounde: Poliphe. It were a well geuen blowe that wolde aduauntage hym. xx. by my trouthe and he eſcaped ſo he myght ſay he roſe vpon his ryght ſyde, but it were maruayle & I cut not of his head harde by his ſhulders. Canni. Yea but good felowe thy goſpell boke teacheth the to geue gentle anſwers, and fayze wozdes

agayne

agayne foz fowle, and to hym that geueth the a blowe vpon the ryght cheke
to holde fozth the lyfte. Poliphe. J do
remembze J haue red fuche a thinge in
my boke,but ye muft pardone me foz J
had quyte fozgotten it. Can. well go
to,what faye ye to pzayer J fuppofe ye
pzaye very ofte.Polt.That is eupn as
very a touche of a pharefey as any can
be.Cannius.J graunt it is no leffe thē
a poynte of a pharefey to pzaye longe
and faynedly vnder a colour oz pzetēce
of holynes, that is to faye when aman
pzayeth not frō the bothum of his hart
but with the lyppes only and from the
tethe outward,and that in opyn places
where great refozt of people is,bycaufe
they wold be fene.But thy gofpel boke
teacheth the to pzaye contynually, but
fo that thy pzayer come from the bothū
of the hart.Polt.Zea but yet foz all my
fayenge J pzaye funityme.Can.when
J befeche the when ÿ art a flepe? Polt.
when it cometh in to my mynde, ones
                    B.ii.   oz

211

oz twyse may chaunce in a weke. Can.
what prayer sayst thou? Poliphe. The
lozdes prayer, the Pater noster. Canni.
Howe many tymes ouer? Poli. Onis, &
I trowe it is often inoughe, foz the gos
pell fozbyddeth often repetynge of one
thynge. Canni. Can ye saye your pater
noster thzough to an ende & haue youre
mynde runnynge vpon nothynge elles
in all that whyle? Poli. By my trouthe
and ye wyll beleue me I neuer yet as=
sayed noz pzoued whether I coulde do
it oz no. But is it not sufficient to saye
it with my mouthe? Can. I can not tell
whether it be oz no. But I am sure god
here vs not excepte we pzaye from the
bothum of our harte. But tell me ano=
ther thyng I wyll aske the. Doest thou
not fast very often? Poli. No neuer in
all my lyfe tyme and yf it were not foz
lacke of meate. Can. And yet thy boke
alowes and commendes hyghly bothe
fastynge and prayer. Polip. So coulde
I alowe them to but that my belly can
not

not well assare noz away with fastyng.
Canni⁹. Yea but Paule sayth they are
not the seruauntes of Jesus Chzsste
whiche serue theyz belly ₰ make it theyz
god. Do you eate flesche every day? Po.
No neuer when J haue none to eate,
but J neuer refuse it when it is set be=
foze me, and J neuer aske question not
foz cōscience but foz my belly sake. Can.
Yea but these stronge sturdy sydes of
suche a chusse and a lobbynge lobye as
thou arte wolde be fed well inoughe ẅ
haye and barke of trees. Poliphe. Yea
but chzyste sayd, that which entereth in
at the mouthe desyleth not the man.
Canni. That is to be vnderstand thus
yf it be measurably taken, and without
the offendinge of our chzistian bzother.
But Paule the disciple of chzyst had ra
ther perysche ₰ sterue with hunger then
onys to offende his weyke bzothzen ẅ
his eatynge, and he exhozteth vs to fol
lowe his example that in all thynges
we maye please all men. Polt, ẅhat tel
                                    ye me

213

ye ma of Paule, Paule is Paule and I am I. Canni⁹. Do you gladly helpe to releue the pooꝛe and the indygent with your goodes? Poli. Howe can I helpe them whiche haue nothynge to gyue them, and scant inoughe foꝛ my selfe. Cannius. ye myght spare somthynge to helpe thē with yf thou woldest playe the good husband in lyuynge moꝛe wa rely, in moderatynge thy superfluous expenses, and in fallynge to thy woꝛke lustely. Poliphem⁹. Nay then I were a fole in dede, a penywoꝛth of ease is euer woꝛth a peny, and nowe I haue found so moch pleasure in ease that I can not fall to no labour. Canni. Do you kepe the commaundementes of god? Polip. Nowe ye appose me, kepe the cōmaundementes ꝙ he, that is a payne in dede. Cannius. Art thou soꝛy foꝛ thy synnes and thyne offences, doest thou ernestly repent the foꝛ thē. Poliphemns. Chꝛist hath payed the raunsome of synne and satisfied foꝛ it alreoy. Cannius. Howe pꝛoupst

214

pꝛoueſt thou then that thou loueſt the
goſpell and fauoꝛis the woꝛd of god as
thou beareſt men in hande thou doeſt.
Poliphemus. I wyll tell you that by ⁊
by, and I dare ſaye you wyl confeſſe no
leſſe your ſelfe then that I am an erneſt
fauoꝛer of the woꝛde when I haue told
you ẏ tale. There was a certayne gray
ſrere of the oꝛder of ſaynt Fraunces w̔
vs whiche neuer ceaſed to bable and
rayle agaynſte the newe teſtament of
Eraſmus, I chaunſed to talke with the
gẽtylman pꝛyuatly where no man was
pꝛeſent but he and I, and after I had
communed awhyle with hym I caught
my ſrere by the polled pate with my left
hande and with my right hãde I dꝛew
out my daggar and I pomelled the
knaue ſrere welfauardly aboute his
ſkonce that I made his face as ſwollen
and as puffed as a puddynge. Canni⁹.
what a tale is this that thou telleſt me.
Poliphemus. How ſay you is not this
a good and a ſufficient pꝛoue that I fa
uer

215

uer the gospell. I gaue hym absolucion
afoze he departed out of my handes w
this newe testament thzyse layde vpon
his pate as harde as I myght dzyue ȳ
I made thze bunches in his heed as
bygge as thze egges in the name of the
father, the sone, ā the holy goost. Can.
Now by my trouth this was well done
ā lyke a ryght gospeller of these dayes.
Truly this is as they saye to dyffende
the gospell with the gospell. Poliphe.
I met another graye frere of the same
curryshe couent, that knaue neuer had
done in raylynge agaynst Erasmus, so
sone as I had espyed hym I was styz-
red and moued with the bzenninge zele
of the gospell that in thzetenyng of him
I made hym knele downe vpon his
knees and crye Erasmus mercie and de
syzed me to forgyue him, I may saye to
you it was hyghe tyme foz hym to fall
downe vpon h.s marybones, and yf he
had not done it by and by I had my hal
barde

barde vp redy to haue gyuen hym be=
twyrt the necke and the heade, I loked
as grymme as modie Mars when he
is in furyous fume, it is trewe that I
tell you, foz there was inoughe sawe
the frere and me yf I wolde make a lye.
Canni⁹. I maruayle the frere was not
out of his wyt. But to retourne to oure
purpose agayne, dost thou lyue chastly?
Poliphemus. Peraduenture I maye
do here after when I am moze stryken
in age. But shall I confesse the trouche
to the? Canni. I am no pzeest man, ther
foze yf thou wylt be shzyuen thou must
seke a pzeest to whome thou maye be
lawfully confessed. Poliphe. I am wont
styl to côfesse my selfe to god, but I wyl
confesse thus moche to the at this tyme
I am not yet become a perfyte gospel=
ler oz an euangelical man, foz I am but
yet as it were one of ÿ cômune people,
ye knowe wel perde we gospellers haue
iiii. gospels wzytten by the. iiii. euange
lystes,

lyftes, & fuche gofpellers as I am hunt
bufely, and chefely for .iiii. thynges that
we may haue. Unde. to proupde dayn=
tie fare for the bellie, that nothynge be
lackynge to that parte of the body whi=
che nature hath placed vnder the belly,
ye wote what I meane, and to obtayne
and procure fuche liuinge that we may
lyue welthely and at pleafure without
carke & care. And fynally that we maye
do what we lyft without checke or con=
trolment, yf we gofpellars lacke none
of all thefe thynges we crye and fynge
for ioye, amonge our ful cuppes Io Io
we tryumphe and are wonderfull fro=
lycke, we fynge and make as mery as
cup and can, and faye the gofpell is a
lyue agayne Chryft rayneth. Cannius.
This is a lyfe for an Epycure or a god
belly and for no euangelicall perfone
that profeffeth the gofpell. Polt. I de=
nye not but that it is fo as ye faye, but
ye knowe well that god is omnipotent
and can do al thynges, he can turne vs
when

whē his wyll is sodenly in to other ma
ner of men. Cannius. So can he trans=
forme you in to hogges and swyne, the
whiche maye soner be done I iudge thē
to chaunge you in to good men for ye
are halfe swynyshe & hoggyshe alredy,
your lyuynge is so beastlie. Poliphe.
Holde thy peas mā wolde to god there
were no men that dyd more hurt in the
worlde then swyne, bullockes, asses, and
camelles. A mā may se many men now
adayes more crueller then lyons, more
rauenynge thē wolues, more lecherous
then sparous, and that byte worse then
mad dogges, more noysom thē snakes,
vepers and adders. Canni⁹. But nowe
good Polipheme remembre and loke
vpon thy selfe for it is hyghe tyme for
the to laye a syde thy beastly lyuynge,
and to be tourned from a brute and a sa
uage beast in to a man. Poliphem⁹. I
thanke you good neyghbour Cannius
for by saynt Mary I thynke your coun=
sayle is good/for the prophetes of this
tyme

tyme ſayth the woꝛlde is almoſt at an end, and we ſhall haue domes daye (as they call it) ſhoꝛtelp. Canni⁹. We haue therfoꝛe moꝛe nede to ſpare our ſelues in a redines agaynſt that day, and that with as moche ſpede as maye be poſſible. Poliphemus. as foꝛ my part I loke and wapte ſtyll euery day foꝛ the myghty hande and power of chꝛiſt. Cannius. Take hede therfoꝛe that thou, when chꝛiſt ſhall laye his myghty hande vpon the be as tendꝛe as waxe, that accoꝛdynge to his eternall wyll he maye frame & faſhyon the with his hande. But wherby I pꝛaye the dothe theſe pꝛophetes coniecture & gather that the woꝛlde is almoſt at an ende. Poliphe. Bycauſe men (they ſape) do the ſelfe ſame thinge nowe adayes that they dyd, and were wont to do which were lyuynge in the woꝛlde a lytle whyle befoꝛe the deluge oꝛ Noyes floode. They make ſolempne feaſtes, they banket, they quaffe, they booll, they bybbe, they ryot men mary,

women

220

wome are marped,they go a catterwal=
lynge and ho3ehuntinge,they bye,they
fell, they lend to vferie, and bo3owe vp
on vferie,they builde,kiges kepe warre
one agaynft another, p3eeftes ftudie
howe they maye get many benefyces
and p3omociõs to make them felke riche
and increafe they3 wo3ldly fubftaunce,
the diuynes make infoluble fillogifmus
and vnperfyte argumētes, they gather
conclufyons, monkes and freers rûne,
at rouers ouer all the wo3ld,the compn
people are in a mafe o3 a hurle burle re
dy to make infurrections, and to con=
clude b3euelie there lackes no éupll mí=
ferie no3 myfchefe,neyther hõger,thy3ft
fellonie,robberie,warre, peftilence,fedi
ctõ,derth,and great fcarfytie and lacke
of all good thynges.And howe fay you
do not all thefe thynges argue and fu=
fficientlie p3oue that the wo3lde is al=
moft at an ende? Cannius.Yea but tell
me I p3aye the of all thes hoole hepe of
eupls and miferies whiche greueth the
moſte?

moste? Poliphemus. whiche thynkes
thou, tell me thy fansie and coniecture?
Cannius. That the Deuyll (god saue
vs) maye daunce in thy purse for euer
a crosse that thou hast to kepe hi for the.
Poliphe. I pray god I dye and yf thou
haue not hyt the nayle vpon the head.
Now as chaunceth I come newly from
a knotte of good companye where we
haue dronke harde euery man for his
parte, & I am not behynde with myne,
and therfore my wytte is not halfe so
fresshe as it wyll be, I wyll dyspute of
the gospell with the whan I am sobre.
Canni. when shal I se the sobre? Polt.
When I shall be sobre. Cannius. whē
wyll that be? Poliph. when thou shalt
se me, in the meane season god be with
you gentle Cannius and well mot you
do. Cannius. And I wyshe to you a
gayne for my parte that thou ware in
dede as valiaunt or pusaunt a felowe
as thy name soundeth. Poliphe. And
bycause ye shall lose nothynge at my
hande

hande with wythynge I pray god that
Cannius maye neuer lacke a good can
o2 a stoope of wyne o2 bere, wherof he
had his name.

F I N I S

The dialoge of thynges and names.

A declaracion of the names.

BEatus, is he whiche hathe abun
dance of al thinges that is good,
and is parfyte in all thynges commen=
dable o2 p2ayseworthy o2 to be desy2ed
of a good man. Somtyme it is ta=
ken fo2 fo2tunate, ryche, o2
noble. Bonifaci⁹, fay2e,
full of fauo2 o2 well
fauo2ed.

The

¶ The parsons names are
Beatus and Bonifacius.

Eatus. God saue you may
ster Boniface. Bonifaci⁹.
God saue you & god saue
you agayne gētle Beatus.
But I wold god bothe we
were such, and so in very dede as we be
called by name, that is to say thou riche
& I fayze. Beatus. why do you thynke
it nothynge wozth at al to haue a good
ly glozious name. Bonifacius. Truely
me thynke it is of no balure oz lytle
good wozthe, onles a man haue the
thynge it selfe whiche is sygnisied by
the name. Beatus. Yea you maye well
thynke your pleasure, but I am assured
that the most part of all moztall men be
of another mynde. Bonifa. It may wel
be I do not denye that they are moztal,
but suerly I do not byleue that they are
me, which are so beastly mynded. Bea.
Yes good syz and they be men to laye
                                                    your

224

your lyfe, onlesse ye thynke camels and
esses do walke aboute vnder the fy=
gure and forme of men. Boni. Mary
I can soner beleue that then that they
be men whiche esteme and passe more
vpon the name, then the thynge. Bea. I
graunte in certayne kyndes of thinges
moost men had rather haue the thynge
then the name, but in many thynges it
is otherwyse and cleane cótrary. Bo. I
can not well tell what ye meane by that
Bea. And yet the example of this matter
is apparant or sufficiently declared in
vs two. Thou arte called Bonifacius
and thou hast in dede the thynge wher=
by thou bearest thy name. yet if there
were no other remedy but eyther thou
must lacke the one or the other, whether
had you rather haue a fowle and defor=
med face or elles for Boniface be called
Maleface or horner? Boni. Beleue me I
had rather be called fowle Thersites
then haue a monstrous or a deformyd
face. whether I haue a good face or no

C.i.   I can

I can not tell .Bea. And euen so had I
foz yf I were ryche and there were no re
medy but that I muſt eyther foggoo my
rycheſſe,oz my name I had rather be cal
led Irus whiche was a pooze beggers
name then lacke my ryches. Boni. I a=
gree to you foz aſmoch as ye ſpeake the
trouth,and as you thynke.Bea. Iudge
all them to be of the ſame mynde that
I am of whiche are indued with helthe
oz other commodities and qualities ap
partaynynge to the body.Boni.That is
bery trewe.Bea.Yea but I pzaye the cõ=
ſyder and marke howe many men we ſe
whiche had rather haue the name of a
lerned and a holy man, then to be well
lerned,bertuous,& holy in dede.Boni.I
knowe a good ſozte of ſuche men foz my
part.Bea.Tell me thy fãtaſie I pzay the
do not ſuche men paſſe moze bpon the
name then the thinge?Boni.Methynke
thy do. Bea. Yf we had a logician here
whiche could well and clarkelie deſyne
what were a kynge, what a byſchoppe,
what

what a magiſtrate, what a philoſopher
is, paduēture we ſhuld find ſom amõg
theſe iolly felowes whiche had rather
haue the name then the thynge. ᴮᵒⁿⁱ.
Surely ⁊ ſo thynke I. Yf he be a kinge
whiche by lawe and equyte regardes
moʒe the commoditie of his people then
his owne lucre/ yf he be a biſſhop which
alwayes is careful foʒ the loʒdes flocke
cõmytted to his paſtoʒall charge/ yf he
be a magiſtrate which frankelie and of
good wyll dothe make pʒouyſyon, and
dothe all thinge foʒ the comyn welthes
ſake/ and yf he be a phyloſopher whiche
paſſynge not vpon the goodes of this
woʒlde, only geueth hym ſelfe to attayn
to a good mynde, and to leade a ver=
tuous lyfe. ᴮᵉᵃ. Lo thus ye may perſey=
ue what a nombʒe of ſemblable exãples
ye may collecte ⁊ gether. ᴮᵒⁿⁱ. Vndou=
ted a great ſoʒte. ᴮᵉᵃ. But I pʒay the tel
me wyll you ſaye that all theſe are no
men. ᴮᵒⁿⁱ. Nay I feare rather leſt in ſo
ſayenge it ſhulde coſt vs our lyues, and

C.ii.   ſo

so myght we our selues shortelye be no men. Bea. Yf man be a resonable crea= ture, howe ferre dyffers this from all good reason, that in cōmodities aper= tayning to the body(for so they deserue rather to be called then goodnes) and in outwarde gyftes whiche dame for= tune geues and takes awaye at her ple asure, we had rather haue the thynge then the name, and in the true and only goodnes of the mynd we passe more vp on the name then the thynge. Boni. So god helpe me it is a corrupte and a pre= posterours iudgement, yf a man marke and consyder it wel. Bea. The selfe same reason is in contrarie thinges. Boni. I wolde gladly knowe what ye meane by that. Bea. We maye iudge lykewyse the same of the names of thynges to be eschued, and incommodites which was spoken of thynges to be dyssyred and cō modites. Boni. Nowe I haue considered the thynges well, it apereth to be euen so as ye saye in dede. Bea. It shulde be more

moze feared of a good pzynce to be a ty
raunt in dede then to haue the name of
a tyzaunt. And yf an euyll byſſhop be a
thefe and a robber, then we ſhulde not
ſo greatly abhozre and hate the name
as the thynge. Boni. Eyther ſo it is oz ſo
tt ſhuld be. Bea. Nowe gather you of
the reſt as I haue done of the pzynce &
the byſſhop. Boni. Me thynkes I vnder=
ſtande this gere wonderouſewell. Bea.
Do not all men hate the name of a fole
oz to be called a moome, a ſotte, oz an
aſſe? Boni. Yeas as moche as they do
any one thynge. Bea. And how ſaye you
were not he a ſtarke fole that wold fiſhe
with a goldē bayte, that wolde pzeferre
oz eſteme glaſſe better then pzecious ſto
nes, oz whiche loues his hozſe oz dog=
ges better then his wyfe and his chyl=
dzē? Boni. He were as wyſe as waltoms
calfe, oz madder then iacke of Redyng.
Bea. And be not they as wyſe whiche
not aſſygned, choſen, noz yet ones ap=
poynted by the magiſtrates, but vpon
theyz

theyz owne heed aduenture to runne to
the warres foz hoope of a lytle gayne,
ieoperdynge theyz bodyes and daunge
rynge theyz foules? Oz howe wyfe be
they which bufie thē felfe to get, glepne,
and reepe to gyther, goodes and ryches
when they haue a mynde deftitute and
lackyng all goodnes? Are not they alfo
euen as wyfe that go gozgyoufly appa
rylled, and buyldes goodly fumptuous
houfes, when theyz myndes are not re
garded but neglect fylthye and with all
kynde of vyce fowle cozrupted? And
how wyfe are they whiche are carefull
diligent and bufie, about the helthe of
theyz body neglectynge and not myn=
dynge at all theyz foule, in daunger of
fo many deedly fynnes? And fynally to
conclude howe wyfe be they whiche foz
a lytle fhozte tranfytozye pleafure of
this lyfe deferue euerlaftynge tozmen=
tes and punyfhementes? Boni. Euen re=
afon fozfeth me to graunt that they are
moze then frātyke and folyfhe. Bea. Yea
but

but althoughe all the whole worlde be
full of suche fooles, a man can scaselye
fynde one whiche can abyde the name
of a foole,and yet they deserue to be cal
led so for asmoche as they hate not the
thynge. Bonf. Suerly it is euen so as ye
seye. Bea. Ye knowe also howe the na=
mes of a lyar and a thefe are abhorred
and hated of all men. Bont. They are
spyteful and odious names, and abhor
red of all men, and not withe out good
cause why. Bea. I graunte that, but al=
thoughe to commyt adulterte be a more
wycked synne then thefte yet for al that
some men retoyse and shewe them selfe
glad of that name,whiche wolde be re=
dy by and by to drawe theyr swerdes
and fyghte withe a man that wolde or
durst call them theues. Bonf. It is true
there are many wolde take it euyll as
you saye in dede. Bea. And nowe it is
commyn to that poynt that thoughe
there are many vnthryftes and spedals
whiche consume theyr substaunce at the
wyne

231

wyne and vpon harlottes, and yet so
wyllynge to continewe openly that all
the worlde wonders at them, yet they
wyll be offended and take peper in the
noose yf a man shulde call them ruffy=
ans oz baudy knaues. Boni. Suche fel=
lowes thynke they deserue prayse foz
the thynge, and yet foz all that they can
not abyde the name dewe to the thinge
whiche they deserue. Bea. There is scar=
slye any name amonges vs moze intol
lerable oz worse can be abydden then to
be called a lyar oz a lyeng fellowe. Boni.
I haue knowen some oz this whiche
haue kylled men foz suche a spytefull
wozde as that is. Bea. Yea yea but
wolde god suche hasty fellowes dyd as
well abhozre the thinge and hate lienge
as well as to be called lyers, was it
neuer thy chaunce to be dyscepued of a=
ny man whiche bozowinge mony of the
appoyntynge the a certayne daye to re=
paye the sayd money and so perfozmyd
not his appoyntment noz kept his daye
Boni.

Boni. Yeas many tymes (god know=
eth) and yet hath he sworne many a gre
uous othe and that not one tyme but
many tymes. Bea. Peraduenture he
wolde haue ben so honest as to haue
payed it and yf he had had wherwith.
Boni. Naye that is not so for he was a=
ble inoughe, but as he thought it better
neuer to paye his dettes. Bea. And
what call you this in englyshe, is it not
playne lyenge? Boni. Yes as playne
as Dunstable waye, there can not be a
lowder lye then this is. Bea. Durste
you be so bolde to pulle one of these
good detters of yours by the sleue and
saye thus to hym, why hast thou dyscep
ued me so many tymes and broken pro
myse with me, or to talke to hym in pla=
yne englyshe, why doest thou make me
so many lyes? Boni. Why no syr by my
trouthe durst I not, excepte I were myn
ded before to chaūge halfe a dosen drye
blowes with hym. Bea. Dothe not ma
sons, Brickelayers, Carpenters, Smy=
thes,

thes, Goldsmithes, Taylours, disceyue
and disapoynt vs after the lyke maner
daylye promysynge to do youre worke
suche a daye and suche a daye without
any fayle, or further delaye, and yet for
all that they parforme not theyr pro-
messe althoughe it stande the neuer so
moche vpon hande, or that thou shul-
dest take neuer so moche profyte by it.
Bont. This is a wonderous and stran
ge vnshamefast knauerye of all that e-
uer I hard of. But and ye speake of bre-
akers of promyse then ye maye reken a
mongest them lawyers and atturneys
at the lawe, which wyl not stycke to pro
myse or beare you in hande that they
wyll be diligent and ernest in the fur-
theraūce and spedie expedicion of your
sute. Bea. Reken ꝙ he, naye ye maye
reken syue hundreth mennes names be
syde these of sundrye faculties and occu
pacions whiche wyll promyse more by
an ynche of a candle then they wyll per
forme by a whole pounde. Bont. Why
and

and ye call this lyenge all the wozlde is full of suche lyenge. Bea. Ye se also lykewyse that no man can abyde to be called thefe, and yet all men do not ab=hozre the thynge so greatly. Boni. I wolde gladly haue you to declare your mynde in this moze playnlye & at large Bea. What difference is there betwene hym whiche stealeth thy money fozthe of thy cofer, and hym whiche fozswea=reth and falsely denyeth that whiche thou cōmytted to his cuftodie to be re=serued and safely kept foz thy vse only, oz to suche tyme as thou arte mynded to call foz it agayne. Boni. There is as they say neyther barrell better hearing, but that in my iudgement he is the fal=ser knaue of the twayne whiche robbes a man that puttes his confidence and truft in hym. Bea. yea but howe fewe men are there nowe adayes lyuynge whiche are contente to reftoze agayne that whiche they were put in truste to kepe, oz yf they delyuer it agayne it is so

so dymynysshed, gelded, nypped, and
pynched, that it is not delyuered whol=
lye, but some thinge cleues in theyr fyn
gers, that the prouerbe may haue place
where the horse walloweth there lyeth
some heares. Boni. I thynke but a
fewe that dothe otherwyse. Bea. And
yet for all that there is none of al these
that cã abyde it ones to be called these,
and yet forsothe they hate not the thing
so greatly. Boni. That is as trewe as
the gospell. Bea. Consyder me nowe
and marke I beseche the howe the goo=
des of orphanes, pupylls, wardes, and
fatherlesse chyldren be cõmuuely orde=
red and vsed, how wylles and testamen
tes be executed and performed, how le=
gacyes and bequethes be communelye
payde, Naye howe moche cleueth and
hangeth fast in the fyngers of the execu
tors or with them that mynyster and in
termedle with the goodes of the testa=
tours. Boni. Many tymes they retay=
ne and kepe in theyr handes all togy=
ther

236

ther. *Bea.* Yea they loue to playe the thefe well inoughe, but they loue nothynge worse then to here of it. *Bont.* That is very trewe. *Bea.* Howe lytle Dyffers he from a thefe whiche borow eth money of one and other and so runneth in dette, with this intent and pur pose that yf he maye escape so or fynde suche a crafty colour or a subtyle Shyft, he intendeth neuer to paye that he ow eth. *Bont.* Paraduenture he maye be called water or more craftier then a thefe is in dede but no poynt better, for it is hard chosyng of a better where there is neuer a good of them bothe. *Bea.* yea but althoughe there be in euery place a great nombre of such makeshyf tes and slypper marchauntes yet the starkest knaue of them all can not abyde to be called thefe. *Bont.* God onely knoweth euery mānes hart and mynd, and therfore they are called of vs men that are runne in dette or fer behynde the hande, but not theues for that soundeth

deth vnswetely and lyke a playne song
note. Bea. What skyllys it howe they
be called amõge men yf they be theues
afoze god. And where you say that god
onely knoweth euery mannes hart and
mynde, euen so euery man knoweth his
owne mynde, whether in his wozdes &
doynges he entende fraude, coupn, dys-
ceyte, and thefte oz no. But what say ye
by hym whiche when he oweth moze
then he is wozthe, wyll not stycke to
lashe pzodygallye and set the cocke vpon the hoope, and yet yf he haue any
money at all lefte to spende that awaye
vnthzyftely, and when he hathe played
the parte of a knauyshe spendall in one
cytie deludinge and disceyuyng his cre-
ditours, ronnes out of this countre
and getteth hym to some other good
towne, and there sekynge foz straũgers
and newe acquayntãce whom he may
lykewyse begyle, yea and playeth many
suche lyke partes and shameful shiftes.
J pzaye the tell me dothe not suche a
greke

greke declare euydentlye by his crafty dealynge and false demeanour, what mynde is he of? Boni. yes suerly as euydentlye as can be possible. But yet suche felowes are wonte to colour and cloke theyr doynges vnder a craftie pretence. Bea. With what I beseche the? Boni. They saye to owe moche and to dyuers persones is communely vsed of great men, yea and of kynges also as well as of them, and therfore they that intende to be of that disposycyon wyll beare out to the harde hedge the porte of a gentylman and soo they wyll be taken and estemed for gentilmen of the commune people. Bea. A gentylman and why or to what entent and purpose a gentylman? Boni. It is a straunge thynge to be spoken howe moche they thynke it is mete for a gentylnan or a horseman to take vpon hym. Bea. By what equytie, authoritie, or lawes. Boni. By none other but by the selfe same lawes that the Admiralles of the

sees

ſees chalenge a propꝛiettie in all ſuche thynges as are caſt bpon the ſhooꝛe by wꝛacke, althoughe the ryghte owner come foꝛthe and chalenge his owne goodes. And alſo by the ſame lawes that ſome other men ſaye all is theyꝛs what ſoeuer is founde aboute a thefe oꝛ a robber whēhe is takē. Bont Such lawes as theſe are the arranteſt theues that are myght make them ſelues. Bea, pea and ye may be ſure they wold gladly w al theyꝛ harts i their bodies make ſuche lawes yf they coulde mayntayne them oꝛ were of power to ſe them execu ted, and they myght haue ſome thynge to laye foꝛ theyꝛ excuſe if they could pꝛo clayme opyn warre befoꝛe they fell to robbynge. Bont. But who gaue that pꝛyuylege rather to a hoꝛſeman then to a foteman, oꝛ moꝛe to a gentylman thē to a good yeman. Bea. The fauoure that is ſhewed to men of warre, foꝛ by ſuche ſhyftes and thus they pꝛactyſe be foꝛe to be good men of warre that they maye

240

maye be moꝛe redy & hanſome to ſpoyle
theyꝛ enemyes when they ſhall encoun=
ter with thē. Bont. J thynke Pyꝛhus
dyd ſo exercyſe and bꝛeake his yonge
ſouldyers to the warres. Bea. No not
Pyꝛrhus but the Lacedemonians dyd.
Bont. Mary ſyꝛ hange vp ſuche pꝛac=
tyſers oꝛ ſoldyers and theyꝛ pꝛactiſyng
to. But howe come they by the name of
hoꝛſemen oꝛ gentylmen that they vſur=
pe ſuche a great pꝛerogatyue? Bea.
Some of them are gentylmē boꝛne and
it cometh to them by aunceſtrie, ſome
bye it by the meanes of mayſtrys mo=
ney, and other ſome gette it by certayne
ſhyftes. Bont. But maye euery man
that wyl and lyſt come by it by ſhyftes?
Bea. Yea why not, euery man maye be
a gentylman nowe adayes very well
and yf theyꝛ condicions and maners be
accoꝛdynge. Bont. What maners oꝛ
condicions muſt ſuche one haue J be=
ſeche the? Bea. Yf he be occupyed a=
boute no goodneſſe, yf he can ruffle it

and swashe in his satens and his silkes
and go gozgiously apparelled, pf he can
ratle in his rynges vpon the fyngers
endes, pf he can playe the ruffyan and
the hozemonger and kepe a gaye hooze
gallantlye, pf he be neuer well at ease
but when he is playenge at the dyse, pf
he be able to matche as moche an vn=
thzpfte as hym selfe with a newe payze
of cardes, pf he spende his tyme lyke an
eppcure vpon bankettinge, sumptuous
fare, and all kynde of pleasures, pf he
talke of no rascalles noz beggars, but
bzagge, bost, face, bzace, and crake of
castelles, towers, and skyzmysshes, and
pf all his talke be of the warres and blo
dy battels, and playe the parte of crac=
kinge Thzaso thzoughly, such gaye gre
kes, lusty bzutes and ionkers may take
vpon them to be at defyaunce withe
whome they wyll and lyst, though the
gentylman haue neuer a fote of lande
to lyue vpon. Boni. Call ye them hozs=
men. Mary syz suche hozsemen are wel
wozthy

worthy to ryde vpō the gallowes, these
are gentylmen of the Iebet of all that
euer I haue harde of. Bea. But yet
there be not afewe suche in that parte
of Germany called Nassen or Hessen.

F   I   N   I   S

Trāslated by Edmonde Becke
And prynted at Cantorbury
in saynt Paules parishe
by Iohñ Mychell.

✠

✠ A mery Dia-
logue, declaringe the proper=
tyes of shrowde shrewes, and honest wyues, not onelie verie
pleasaunte, but also not a
lytle profitable: made
by þ famous clerke
D. Erasmus
Roteroda=
mus.
Translated in to
Englyshe.
⚘ * ⚘
⁂

¶Anno.M.CCCCC.
LVII.

245

Ulalia.God spede,& a thou
sand mine old acqueintāce.
xantippa.xan. As many a=
gayn,my dere hert.Eulalf.
me semets ye ar waxē much faire now
of late.Eula. Saye you so? gyue you
me a mocke at the first dash.xan. Nay
berzly but I take you so.Eula. Hap=
pely mi new gown maketh me to loke
fayzer then I sholde doe. xan. So the
you saye, I haue not sene a mynioner
this many dayes, I reken it Englishe
cloth.Eu. It is english stuff and dyed
in Uenis.xan. It is softer then sylke
what an oziente purpel coloze here is
who gaue you so rich a gift. Eu.How
shoulde honeste women come by their
gere?but by their husbandes.xā.Hap
py arte thou that hathe suche an husband, but I wolde to god for his pas=
syon, that I had maryed an husband
of clowts,when I had maried col my
good mā.Eula.Why say,ye so.I pzay
you. are you at oddes now.xā. I shal
neuer be at one w̄ him ye se how beg=

gerly I go. I haue not an hole smock to put on my backe,and he is wel contente with all: I praye god I neuer come in heuen & I be not aschamed oftimes to shewe my head,when I se other wiues how net and trim they go that ar matched with farre porer mē then he is. Eula. The apparell of honest wiues is not in the aray of the body,noz in the tirementes of their head as saynte Peter the apostle teacheth vs(and that I learned a late at a sermon)but in good lyuynge and honest conuersacion and in the oznamentes of the soule,the cōmon buenes ar painted vp, to please manye mennes eies we ar trime ynough yf we please our husbands only,xan.But yet my good man so eupll wylling to bestow oughe vpon his wyfe, maketh good chere, and lassheth out the dowzye that hee hadde with mee no small pot of wine. Eulaly,where vpon.xantipha,wheron hym lykethe beste, at the tauerne, at the stewes,and at the dyce.Eulalia

Peace

Peace saye not so. ran. wel yet thus it
is, then when he cōmeth home to me
at midnight, longe watched for, he lyeth rowtyng lyke a sloyne all the leue
longe nyght, yea and now and thē he
all bespeweth his bed, and worse then
I will say at this tyme, Eulali. Peace
thou dyshonesteth thy self, when thou
doest dishonesteth thy husbād. rantip.
The deuyl take me bodye and bones
but I had leuer lye by a sow with pig-
ges, then with suche a bedfelowe. Eulali. Doest thou not then take him vp,
wel fauoredly for stūbling. rantip. As
he deserueth I spare no tonge. Eulali
a. what doth he thē. rantip. At the first
breake he toke me vp vengeably, tru-
sting that he shoulde haue shakē me of
and put me to scilence with his crabid
wordes. Eula Came neuer your hote
wordes vnto hādstrokes. rantip. On
a tyme we fel so farre at wordes ꝑ we
wer almost by ꝑ eares togither. Eula
what say you womā. ran. He toke vp
a staffe wandryng at me, as the deuill
hadde

had bene on hym ready to laye me on
the bones. Eula. were thou not redye
to ron in at the bech hole. xanti. Nay
mary I warrant the. I gat me a thre
foted stole in hand, & he had but ones
layd his littell finger on me, he shulde
not haue founde me lame . I woulde
haue holden his nose to the grindstöe
Eulalia. A newe found shelde, ye wan
ted but youre dystaffe to haue made
you a speare. xantip. And he shoulde
not greatlye a laughed at his parte.
Eulali. Ah my frynde. xantyppa. that
way is neither good nor godli, xantip
pa what is neither good nor godly. yf
he wyll not vse me, as hys wyfe: I wil
not take him for my husbande. Eulalya.   But Paule sayeth that wyues
shoulde bec boner and buxume vnto
their husbandes with all humylytye,
and Peter also bryngethe vs an example of Sara, that called her husbande Abrahame, Lorde. xantippa. I
know that as well as you thē $ same
paule say that men shoulde loue theyr
wyues

250

wyues,as Chzist loued his spouse the
churche,let him do his duete I wil do
myne. Eula. But foz all that,when the
matter is so farre that the one muste
fozber the other it is reason that the
woman giue place vnto the man, ran.
Is he meete to be called my husbãde
that maketh me his vnderlynge and
his dzyuel? Eula. But tel me dame xã
tip.Would he neuer offre the stripes
after that xãtip. Not a stripe,and ther
in he was the wyser man foz ã he had
he shoulde haue repented euery vayne
in hys harte. Eulali. But thou offered
him foule wozdes plentie,xantip. And
will do. Eula.What doth he ŷ meane
seasõ. xantip. What doth he sometyme
he cowcheth an hogeshed, somtime he
doth nothing but stande and laughe
at me, other whyle takethe hys Lute
wheron is scarslie thzee strynges lay=
enge on that as fast as he may dzyue
because he would not here me. Eula.
Doeth that greue thee? xantippa. To
beyende home, manie a tyme I haue

I iiii   much

251

much a do to hold my handes. Eula.
Neighbour. xantip.wylt thou gyue
me leaue to be playn with the.xantip=
pa Good leaue haue you.Eula.Be as
bolde on me agayne our olde acqnayn
taunçe and amite,euen frō our chyld=
hode,would it should be so. xantippa.
Trueth you saie,there was neuer wo
man kinde that I fauoured moꝛe Ela
ly Whatsoeuer thy husbād be, marke
well this,chaunge thou canst not, In
the olde lawe,where the deuill hadde
cast aboone betwene the man and the
wife,at the woꝛste waye they myght
be deuoꝛsed,but now that remedie is
past,euē till death depart you he must
nedes be thy husbande, and thou hys
wyfe,xan.Il mote they thꝛyue & thei
that taken away that liberty from vs
Eulalia.Beware what thou sayest, it
was chꝛistes act.Xā.I can euil beleue
that Eula.It is none otherwyse,now
it is beste that eyther of you one be=
yng with an other , ye laboure to liue
at reste and peace.xantyppa,   Why=
                                         can

can I forgeue him a new. Eu. It lieth
great parte in the wome, for the ordé
ringe of theyr husbandes. ran. Lea=
dest thou a mery life with thine. Eula
Now all is well. ran. Ergo ther was
somwhat to do at your fyrste metyng
Eula. Neuer no greate busynes, but
yet as it, happeneth now and than be
twene man & womā, there was foule
cloudes a loft, that might haue made
a storme but that they were ouer blo=
wen with good humanitie and wyse
handlynge. Euery man hath hys ma=
ner and euery mā hath his seueral ap
tite or mynde, and thinkes hys owne
way best, & yf we list not to lie there li=
ueth no mā without faulte, which yf a
nie were elles, ywis in wedlocke they
ought to know and not vtterly hated
ran, you say well, Eulalya. It happe=
neth many times that loue dayes bre
keth betwene man and wife, before ȳ
one be perfitly knowé vnto the other
beware of that in any wise, for when
malice is ones begon, loue is but ba=
rely

rely redressed agayne, namelye, yf the
mater grow furthe vnto bytter checkes, & shamfull raylinges such things
as are fastened with glew, yf a manne
wyll all to shake them strayght waye
whyle the glew is warme, they soone
fal in peces, but after ẙ glewe is ones
dried vp they cleue togither so fast as
anie thing, wherfore at the beginning
a meanes must be made, that loue mai
encrease and be made sure betwene ẙ
man & the wife, & that is best brought
aboute by gentilnesse and fayre condy
cions, for the loue that beautie onelie
causeth, is in a maner but a cheri faire
Xan.   But I praye you hartelye tell
me, by what pollycy ye brought your
good man to folow your daunce. Eula. I wyll tell you on this condicyon,
that ye will folowe me. xan. I can. Eu
la, It is as easy as water yf ye cã find
in your hart to do it, nor yet no good
time past for he is a yong mã, and you
ar but a girle of age, and I trowe it is
not a yere ful sins ye wer maried. Xã.
Ill

All thys is true Eulalia, I wyll shew
you then. But you must kepe it secret
rantip, with a ryght good wyl. Eula.
This was my chyefe care, to kepe me
alwayes in my housbandes fauoure,
that there shulde nothyng angre him
I obserued his appetite and pleasure
I marked the tymes bothe whan he
woulde be pleased and when he wold
be all byshrwed, as they tameth the
Elephantes and Lyons or suche beastes that can not be wonne by stregth
rantyppa. Suche a beaste haue I at
home. Eula. Thei that goth vnto the
Elephantes weare no white garmen
tes, nor they that tame wylde bulles,
weare no blasynge reedes, for experience teacheth, that suche beastes bee
madde with those colours, like as the
Tygers by the sounde of tumbrels be
made so wode, that thei plucke theym
selfin peces. Also thei y̆ breake horses
haue their termes and theyr soundes
theyr hadlynges, and other knackes
to breake their wyldnes, wyth all.
                                 How

255

Howe much moze then is it oure due
tyes that ye wyues to vse suche craf=
tes toward our husbandes with whō
all our lyfe tyme wil we,nyl we is one
house,and one bed.rantip.furthwith
youre tale. Eula,whē I had ones mar
ked there thynges. I applied my selfe
vnto hym, well ware not to displease
hym.rantip.How could thou do that.
Eulalya. Fyzste in the ouerseynge my
householde,which is the very charge
and cure of wyues , I wayted euer,
not onely gyuynge hede that nothing
shoulde be fozgotten oz vndoone, but
that althynges shoulde as he woulde
haue it, wer it euer so small a trifle.rā
wherin.Eulalia. Is thus.Yf mi good
man had a fantasye to this thynge, oz
to that thyng, oz if he would haue his
meate dzessed on this fashion, oz that
fashion.ran. But howe couldest thou
fashyon thye selfe after hys wyll and
mynde, that eyther woulde not be at
home.oz elles be as fresshe as a saulte
heryng.Elali.Abyde a while, I come
not

256

not at that yet, yf my husband wer very sad at anye tyme, no time to speake to him. I laughed not nor tryfled him as many a woman doth but I looked rufully and heauyly, for as a glasse (if it be a true stone) representeth euer ȳ physnamy of hym that loketh in it, so lykewyse it becommeth a wedded woman alway to agre vnto the appetite of her husbande, that she be not mery whē he murneth. nor dysposed to play whē he is sad. And if that at any time he be waiward shrewshaken, either I pacyfye hym with faire wordes, or I let hym alone, vntyll the wynde be oueꝛblowen gyuing him neuer a word at al, vntyl the time come that I may eyther excuse my faute, or tell hym of hys. In lykewyse when he commeth home wel whitled, I gyue hym gentyll and fayre woordes, so with fayre entreatynge I gette hym to bed. ran-typpa. O carefull state of wyues, whē they muste be gladde and fayne to fol-lowe their husbandes mindes, be theī cluyshe

clupſhe.dʒonken,oʒ doyng what myſ-
chiefe they liſte.Eula. As whoe ſaieth
this gentill dealynge ſerueth not foʒ
bothe partyes,foʒ they ſpyte of theyʒ
berdes muſte ſuffre many thynges in
our demeanoʒ,yet a time ther is,whē
in a weighty matter it is laufull that
the wyfe tell the good mā his faute, if
that it be matter of ſubſtaunce, foʒ at
lyght trifles,it is beſt to play byll vnder wynge.xantyp.what time is that
Eula.when he is ydle,neither angry,
penſife,noʒ ouerſen.then betwixt you
two ſecretly he muſt be told his faute
gētly,oʒ rather intreated.that in this
thynge oʒ that he play the better huſ-
bande,to loke better to his good name and fame and to his helth and this
tellyng muſt be myxt with mery conceites and pleaſaunt woʒdes many ti
mes J make a meane to tel my tale af
ter this faſhyon,that he ſhall pʒomiſe
me,hee ſhal take no diſpleaſure wyth
my thynge, that J a foolyſhe woman
ſhall bʒeake vnto hym, that pertay-
neth

neth eyther to hys helthe woꝛſhyppe oꝛ welth.Whē I haue ſayde that I woulde,I chop cleane from that com-munication and falle into ſome other paſtime ,foꝛ this is all oure fautes, neyghbour Xantippa,that whē we be gyn ones to chat our tounges neuer lie.Xantip.So men ſay Eulalia.

Thus was I well ware on,that I ne uer tell my huſbād his fautes befoꝛe companie,noꝛ I neuer caried any cō-playnte furthe a doꝛes:the mendes is ſoner made whē none knoweth it but two,and there were anie ſuche faute that myght not be wel boꝛne noꝛ amē ded by ẏ wyues tellige,it is moꝛe lau-dable that the wife make complaynte vnto the Parentes and kynſfolke of her huſband,then vnto her own,and ſo to moderate her complaynte that She ſeme not to hate hym but hys vice noꝛ let her play all the blabbe, that in ſome poynt bnꝛtered,he may know ꝗ loue his wiues curteyſy.Xantip.She had nede be aſwel lerned womā , that
ſſould

ſhould do all this. Eu. Mary through ſuche demeanoure, we ſhall ſterre our huſbādes vnto lyke gentylneſſe. Xan: There be ſome that cannot be amended with all the gentyll handlynge in the worlde. Eula: In faith I thyncke nay, but caſe there be, marke this wel the good man muſt be for borne, howe ſoeuer the game goeth, then is ʒt better to haue him alwayes at one point or ells more kinde and louing throw oure genttil handlinge, then to haue him worſe and worſe throwe our curſedneſſe, what wyll you ſay and I tell you of huſbādes that hath won theyr wiues by ſuche curteſie, howe muche more are we boūde to vſe the ſame to warde our huſbandes. Xantip. Than ſhall you tell of one farre vnlyke vnto thyne huſband. Eula. I am aquented with a certayne gentelman well lerned and a veri honeſt man, he maried a yonge wyfe, a mayden of. xvii. yeare olde brede and brought vp of a chylde in the countre vnder her fathers and

mothers

mother wing (as gentilmen delite to
dwel in the countre) to hunt & hawke
This yong gētilman would haue one
that were vnbꝛokē, becaufe he might
the foner bꝛeake her after hys owne
mind, he begā to entre her in learning
fyngynge, and playinge, and by lytle
and lytle to vfe here to repete fuche
thynges as ſhe harde at fermons, and
to inſtruct her with other things that
myght haue doone her moꝛe good in
time to come. This gere, becaufe it
was ſtraūge vnto this young womā
which at home was bꝛought vp in all
ydelneſſe, and with the light commu=
nication of her fathers feruauntes,
and other paſtimes, begā to waxe gre
uouſe & paynfull, vnto her. She with
dꝛew her good mynde and dylygence
and whē her huſband called vpon her
She put ỹ finger in the eye, and wepte
and many times ſhe would fal downe
on the grounde, beatynge her head a=
gȝ ẏnſt the floure, as one that woulde
be out of thys woꝛlde. When there
B was

was no healpe for this gere, the good
man as though he hadde bene wel as=
ked his wyfe yf she woulde ryde into
the countre with him a sporting vnto
her fathers house, so that she graun=
ted anone. When they were cōme thy
ther, the gentilman left his wyfe with
her mother & her sisters he wēt furth
an huntynge with his father in lawe,
there betwene theym two, he shewed
al together, how that he hadde hoped
to haue had a louynge companion to
lead his lyfe withall, now he hath one
that is alwaies blubberynge and py=
ninge her selfe awaye withoute anye
remedie, he prayeth him to lay to hys
hande in amendinge his doughters
fautes her father answered ꝑ he had
ones giuen hym his doughter, and yf
that she woulde not be rewled by wor
des (a goddes name take Stafforde
lawe) she was his owne. Then the gē
tylman sayd agayne, I knowe that I
may do but I had leuer haue her amē
ded eyther by youre good counsell or
commaun

262

cōmmaundement, then to come vnto
that extreme waies, her father promi
sed that he woulde synde a remedye,
After a dai or two, he espied time and
place whē he might be alone with his
doughter. Then he loked sourelī vpō
his doughter, as though he had bene
horne woode with her, he began to re
herse how foule a beaste she was, how
he feared many tymes that she neuer
haue bestowed her. And yet sayde he
muche a doe, vnto my great coste and
charg, I haue gottē the one that mou
ghte lye by any Ladyes syde, and she
were a quene and yet thou not perset
uynge what I haue done for the nor
knowynge that thou hast suche a man
whiche but of his goodnes myghte
thyncke thee to euill to be stoye in his
kytchen, thou contrariest al his mind
to make a short tale he spake so sharpe
ly to her, that she feared that he wold
haue beaten her, It is a man of a sub-
tyll and wylye wytte, whyche wythout a bysarde is readye to playe anye

maner of parte. Thē this yonge wife
what for feare, and for trouthe of the
matter, cleane stryken oute of counte
naunce, fell downe at her fathers fete
despryng hym that he wolde forgette
and forgiue her all that was past and
euer after she woulde doe her duetye
Her father forgaue her, and promised
that she shoulde finde him a kynd and
a louynge father, yf so be that she per=
fourmed her prompse. rantippa. How
dyd she afterwarde. Eulalya, whē she
was departed frō her father she came
backe into a chaumber, and there by
chaunce found her husband alone she
fel on her knees to hym and said. Mā
in tymes paste, I neyther knewe you
nor my selfe, from this daye froward
ye shall se me cleane chaunged, onelye
pardon that is past, with that her hus
bande toke her in his armes & kyssed
her sayinge she should lacke nothyng
yf she woulde holde her in that mind.
rantip. Why did she cōtinue so. Eula=
lya, Euen tyll her endynge daye. nor
there

264

there was none so vyle a thynge but
that she woulde laye handes on it redely with all her herte, if her husband
wolde let her, so great loue was begō
and assured betwene them and many
a daye after. shee thanked god ȳ euer
she met with such a mā. For yf she had
not she sayd she had ben cleane caste a
waye. xan. We haue as greate plentie
of suche housbandes, as of white crowes. Eulalya. Now, but for werieng
you ꝛ I toulde tell you a thynge that
chaunsed alate in this same citye. xan
typpa. I haue litell to doe, and I lyke
your communicacyon very well. Eulalia. There was a certaine gentilmā
he as suche sort of men do, vsed much
huntyng in the cuntre, where he happened on a younge damoysell, a very
poꝛe womās chuld on whō he doted a
man well stryken in age, and for her
sake he lay oftē out of his owne house
his excuse was hūtig. This mās wife
an exceeding honest womā, halfe deale
suspecte the mater, tried out her husbandes

bandes falshed, on a tyme whē he had taken his iourney sourth of the town vnto some other waies, She wente vn to that poore cotage and boultcd out all the hoole matter, where he laye on nights, wheron he dꝛāke, what thyng thei had to welcō him withall. There was neither one thyng noꝛ other, but bare walles. This good womā retur ned home, and sone after came againe bꝛynginge w her a good soft bed, and al therto belongyng and certain plate besydes that She gaue them moneye, chargynge them that if the Gentilmā came agayne, they Sſould entreate him better not beyng knowē al this while that She was his wyfe, but sayued her to be her sister. Not long after her hus band stale thether againe, he sawe the howse otherwyse decked, and better sare then he was wounte to haue. He asked, frome whence commeth al this goodly gere? They sayde that an ho neste matrone, a kynscwoman of hys hadde bꝛoughte it thyther and com-
                                                maunded

266

maunded them that he would be well
cherished when so euer he came , by
and by his hart gaue him that it was
hys wiues dede, whan he came home
he demaũded of her yf she hadde bene
there oz nay,she sayd yea.Then he asked her foz what purpose she sente all
that housholde stuffe thyther. Man
(said she)ye haue bē tenderly bzought
vp I perceiued that ye were but cozs-
lie handled there,me thought that it
was my part,seing it was your wyll
and pleasure to be there ye shoulde
be better loked to. Xantippa. She
was one of goddes fooles. I woulde
rather foz a bed haue layd bnder him
a bundel of nettels:oz a burden of thi
stels.Eula.But here the end her hus=
bande percepyng the honeste of her
great pacience neuer after laye from
her, but made good cheare at home
with his owne. I am sure y e knowe
Gilberte the holãder.xan.Uery well.
Eu.He(as it is not bnknowē maried
an old wife in his flozishig youth. Xã.
Biut   Her

aduenture he maried the good and not the woman. Eulalia. There sayde ye well, setting lytell stoore by hys olde wife, hunted a callette, with whom he kept much companie abrode, he dined or supped litell at home. What wouldest thou haue sayd to ȳ gere. Xantip. What woulde I a said? I wolde haue flowē to the hoies toppe and I wolde haue crowned mryne husbande at hys oute goinge to her with a pysbowle, that he so ēbawlmed might haue gon vnto his souerayne ladie. Eula. But how much wiselier dyd this woman? She despied that yonge woman home vnto her, and made her good chere, so by that meanes she brought home also her husband without ani witchiaft oi soiserie, and yf that at anye seaſon he supped abrode with her she would sende vnto them some good dayntie moiſel, and byd him make goed chere Xantippa. I had leuer be slayne then I woulde be bawde vnto myne owne husbande. Eulalia. Yes, but conſyder all

all thynges well,was not that muche better, then she shoulde be her shrewyshnesse, haue putte her husbandes minde cleane of from her,and so haue ledde all her life in trouble and heuynesse.Xantippa. I graunte you well, that it was better so but I coulde not abyde it. Eulalya. I wyll tell you a prety story more,and so make an ende One of oure neyghboures,a well disposed and a goddes man , but that he is some what testie, on a day pomeld his wife well and thriftely aboute the pate and so good a woman as euer was borne, she picked her into a inner parler,and there weepynge and sobbynge, eased her heuye harte , anone after, by chaunce her husbande came into the same place , and founde hys wyfe wepyng.What seest thou heare sayth he seighing & sobbig like a child Thē she like a wise womā sayde. Is it not more honesty for me to lamente my dolours here in a secret place,thē to make wondering and on oute crye
in

in the strete, as other womē do. At so
wysely and womanly a saing his hart
melted, promysynge her faythfullye
and truelie that he woulde neuer laye
stroke on her afterwarde, nor neuer
did. Xantippa. No more wil mine god
thanke my selfe. Eulalya. But then ye
are alwates one at a nother, agreinge
lyke dogges and cattes. Xan. What
wouldest thou that I should do. Eu.
Fyrst & formest, whatsoeuer thy husbande doeth sayde thou nothinge, for
his harte must be wonne by lytell and
litel by fayre meanes, gentilnesse and
forbearing at the last thou shalte eyther wynne him or at the leaste waie
thou shalt leade a better life thē thou
doest now. Xantippa. He his beyonde
goddes forbode, he wil neuer amende
Eulalia. Eye saye not so, there is no
beest so wild but by fayre handling be
tamed, neuer mistrust man thē. Assay
a moneth or two, blame me and thou
findest not that my counsell doeth
ease. There be some fautes wyth you
though

270

thoughe thou se them,be wyſe of this
eſpecyall that thou neuer gyue hym
foule woꝛdes in the chambꝛe,oꝛ inbed
but be ſure that all thynges there bee
full of paſtyme and pleaſure. foꝛ yf
that place which is oꝛdeined to make
amides foꝛ all fautes and ſo to renew
loue,be polluted,eyther with ſtrife oꝛ
grudgynges, then fayꝛe wel al hope of
loue daies, oꝛ atonementes,yet there
be ſome beaſtes ſo wayward and mis=
cheuous,that when theyꝛ huſbandes
hath them in their armes a bed, they
ſcholde ⁊ chyde making ꝑ ſame pleſuꝛ
their lewd condicions (that expelſeth
all diſpleaſures oute of their huſban=
des mynde vnpleaſaunt and lytell ſet
bi coꝛrupting the medecine that ſhuld
haue cured al deadly greiſes,⁊ odible
offices. xantip. That is no newes to
me. Eula. Though the woman ſhulde
be well waꝛe and wyſe that ſhe ſhulbe
neuer be diſobedient vnto her huſbãd
yet ſhe ought tobe moſt circũſpect ꝑat
that

that at meting she shew her selfe redy
and pleasaunt vnto him. xantyppa.
Yea vnto a man, holde well withall
but J am combred with a beast. Eula.
No moze of those wozdes, most com
monly our husbades ar euyll through
our owne faute, but to returne againe
vnto our taile they that ar sene in the
olde fables of Poetes sai that Uenus
whome they make chiefe lady of wed
locke (hath a girdle made by the han-
dy wozke of Uulcan her Lozde, and
in that is thzust al that enforceth loue
and with that she girdeth her whan
so euer she lyeth wyth her housbande
xantippa. A tale of a tubbe. Eulalya.
A tayle it is, but herke what the taile
meaneth. xantippa. Tell me. Eulalia
That techeth vs that the wyfe ought
to dyspose her selfe all that she maye
that lieng by her husbad she shew him
al the plesure that she ca. Wherby the
honest loue of matrimony may reuiue
and be renewed, & that there with be
clene dispatched al grudges & malice
xan.

rant.But how shall we come by thys
gyrdle.~Eula. We nede neyther wyt-
chraft nor enchauntment, ther is non
of them al,so sure as honest condiciõs
accompayned with good feloshyp.ran
I can not fauoure suche an husbande
as myne is.Eula, It is moste thy pro
fyt that he be no longer suche.If thou
couldest by thy Circes craft chaunge
thin husband into an hogge, or a bore
wouldest thou do it.~rantip. God kno
weth. Eu. Ert thou in dout.~haddest
thou leauer marye an hogge than a
mã.rantip. Mary I had leauer hauẽ
a manne,Eulalia.wel, what and thou
couldest by sorcery make him of a drõ
karde a soober man, of a vnthrifte a
good housbande of an ydell losell a towarde body,woldest thou not doe it.~
rantip.yes,hardely,woulde I doe it.
But where shoulde I learne the cun-
nyng.~Eula.forsoth that cõning hast
thou in the if thou wouldest vtter it,
thyn must he be,mauger thy head,the
towarde ÿ makest him,the better it is
                                    for

for the, thou lokest on nothing but on his leude cōndicions, and thei make the half mad, thou wouldest amende hym and thou puttest hym farther oute of frame, loke rather on his good condicions, and so shalt thou make him better. It is to late calagayne yesterdaie before thou were maryed vnto hym. It was tyme to cōsyder what his fautes were for a woman shold not only take her husbande by the eyes but by the eares. Now it is more tyme to redresse fautes thē to fynd fautes. xantf. What woman euer tore her gusband by the eares. Eulali. She taketh her husbande by the eyes that loketh on nothyng, but on the beautye and pulcritude of the body. She taketh him by the eares, that harkeneth dilygētly what the common voice sayth by hym xantip. Thy counsaile is good, but it commeth a day after the faire. Eula. Yet it commeth time ynough to brynge thyne husbande to a greate furtheraunce to that shall bee yf God sende you

274

you anie frute togither. Xantippa. We are spede alredy of that. Eulaly. How longe ago. Xantip. A good whyle ago Eulalia. How many monethes old is it. Xantip. It lacketh lytle of. vii. Eula What a tale is this, ye reken the monethes by nightes and dayes double. Xantippa. Not so. Eula. It can not be none otherwyse, yf ye reken from the mariage day. Xantippa. yea, but what thē, I spake with him befoze we were maried. Eulalia. Be childzen gotten by speakinge. Xantip. It befell so that he mette me alone and begon to ticke at me, and tickled me bnder the arme holes and sydes to make me laugh. I might not awaie with ticklynge, but fell downe backewarde bpon a bedde and he a lofte, neuer leuinge kyssynge on me, what he did els I can not saye, but by sayncte Marie within a while after my bely beganne to swell. Eula. Go now and dispzayse thyne husbāde whiche yf he gette childzen by playe, what wyll he do whē he goeth to it in good

good erneſt.xantippa,J fere me J am
payed agayin.Eula.Good·locke God
hath ſent a fruitfull grounde, a good
tylmã.xantip.In that thing he might
haue leſſe laboure and moze thanke.
Eula.few wyues finde at theyz huſbandes in that behalf but were ye the͂
ſure togither.xanti.yea that we were
Eula.The offence is the leſſe. Is it a
man chylde.xantip.yea.Eula.He ſhal
make you at one ſo that ye wil bow &
fozbere.What ſaieth other me͂ by thin
huſband,they that be his cõpanions,
they delite with him abzode xã.They
ſay that he is meruelous gentyl,redy
to do euerp man pleaſure,liberal and
ſure to his frende.Eula.And that put
teth me in good cõfozt that he wyll be
ruled after our counſayll.xantip.But
J fynde him not ſo.Eula. Ozder thy
ſelfe to him as J haue tolde thee, and
cal me no moze true ſayer but a lier,if
he be not ſo good vnto the as to anie
creature liuinge Agayne cõſidze this
he is,yet but a childe,J thinke ye paſ-
ſeth

seethe not. xxiiij. the blacke oxe neuer
trode on hys fote, nowe it is but loste
laboure to recken vpon anye deuorse.
xantippa. Yet manye a tyme and ofte
I haue troubled my braynes with al
Eulalia. As for that fantasye whenso
euer it commeth into your mynd first
of all counte how naked a thynge wo
man is, deuorsed from man. It is the
hyghest dignitie that longethe to the
wyfe to obsequyous vnto her spouse.
So hath nature ordeined so god hath
apoynted, that the woman shoulde be
ruled al by the man loke onely vppon
this whiche is trouth, thine husbande
he is, other canste thou none haue. A-
gaine forgette not that swete babe be
gotten of both your bodies what thin
keste thou to do with that, wilte thou
take it awaye with thee. Thou sha te
berene thyne husband his ryghtwylt
thou leue it with hym, thou shalt spoi
le thy self of thy chefeste Jewell thou
haste.   Beside all this tell mee trueth
hast thou none euyll wyllers. Besyde

all thyg tell me trueth, haſt thou none
eupll wpllers. ran. I haue a ſtepdame
I warrant you, and myne huſbandes
mother euen ſuch another. Eula. Do
they hate the ſo deadly. rantip. They
woulde ſe me hanged. Eula. Thē for-
get not thē, what greater pleſure coul
deſt thou ſhew them then to ſe the de
uorſed from thine huſband and to led
a wydowes lyfe. Yea and worſe thēa
wydow, for wydowes be at their choi
ſe. rantippa. I holde well with youre
coūſell, but I can not awaye wyth the
paynes, Eulalia. yet recken what paines ye toke or ye colde teache your pa
ret to ſpeake. rantippa. Erceadynge
much. Eu. And thinke you much to la
bour a lytel in reforming your huſbād
with whō you may liue merely all the
dayes of your lyfe. What buſines doe
mē put thē ſelf tobe wel & eaſly horſed
& ſhal we think our ſelues to good to
take paines that we mai haue our huſ
bādes gētil & curteiſe vnto vs. rantip
What ſhal I do. Eu, I haue told you
all

al redy, se that al thing be clene & trim
at home, that no sluttysh or vnclenlye
syghtes dryue hym oute a dores. Be
your selfe alwayes redy at a becke, be
rynge continuall in minde what reue
rēce the wife oweth vnto her husbād.
Be neyther in your dumpes, nor alway
es on your mery pinnes go nether to
homely nor to nycely. Let your meat
be cleane dressed, you know your hus-
bādes diet. What he loueth best that
dresse. Moreouer shewe your selfe louinge and fayre spokē vnto thē where
he loueth, call them now and thē vnto your table. At meate, se that al thin
ges be well sauored, and make good
chere, And whē that he is toppe heuy
playing on his lute, sytte thou by and
singe to him so shalte thou make hym
keepe home, and lessen hys expences
This shall he thynke at length, in saythe I am a sonde felowe that maketh
suche chere with a strumpet abroode,
with greate lossee bothe of substance
and name, seyng that I haue a wyfe
C ii   at

at home bothe muche fayzer, and one
that loueth me ten times better, with
whome J may be both clenlyer receiued and dayntelier cherisched rantip.
Beleuest thou that it will take and J
put it into a profe. Eulali.   Looke on
me. J warrante it oz ought longe J
wyll in hande with thyne husbande, A
J will tell hym his parte. rantippa. ye
marie that is well sayde. But be wyse
that he espie not our caste, he would
plaie his sages, all the house should be
to lytle foz hym. Eulalia.   Take no
thoughte. J shall so conuey my matters, that he shall dysclose all together hym selfe, what busynesse is betwene you, that done J wyll handell
him pretelie as J thinke beste, and J
truste to make him a new man foz the
and when Jse my time J wyl make a
lie foz thee, how louinge thou hast spoken of him. rantippa. Chzyst spede vs
and bzinge our pupose well aboute.
Eulalia. He will not fayle the so thou
do thy good wyll

There

Here was a man that maried a woman whiche hadde great riches and beawtye. Howe bee it she hadde suche an impedyment of nature that she was domme and coulde not speake, whiche thynge made him ryghte pensyfe, and sayd, wherfore vpon a daye as he walked alone ryght heuye in hearte thynkynge vpon his wyfe. There came one to hym and asked him what was the cause of his heuynesse whiche answered that it was onely bycause his wife was borne dōme. To whome this other said I shal shewe the soone a remedy and a medityne (therfore that is thus) go tak an aspen leafe and lay it vnder her tōge this night shee bringe a sleape, and I warrant the that shee shall speake on the morowe whiche man beyng glad of thys medycyne prepared therfore and gathered aspen leaues, wherfore he layd thre of them vnder her tonge whan shee was a sleape. And on the

morow when he him selfe awaked, he
desyrous to know how hys medicine
wrought being in bed with her, he demaunded of her how she did, and sodē
ly she answered and sayd, I beshrewe
thy harte for waking me so early, and
so by the vertue of that medycyne she
was restored to her speche. But in cō
clusion her spech encresed day by day
and she was so curst of cōdycyon that
euery date she brauled and chyd with
her husbande, so muche at the laste he
was more greed, and had much more
trouble and disease wyth her shrewed
wordes then he hadde before whē she
was dumme; wherfore as he walked
another time alone he happened to
mete agayne with the same personne
that taught hym the sayde medycine
and sayde to hym thys wyse. Syr ye
taught me a medicin but late to make
my domme wyfe to speake, byddynge
me lay an Aspen leafe vnder her toūg
when she sleapte, and I layde three
Aspen leaues there. Wherfore nowe
she

&c speaketh. But yet &e speaketh soo
much & so shzewdlye that I am moze
werier of her now,then I was when
ste was dōme:Wherfoze I praie you
teache me a medycine to modyfye her
that ste speake not so muche. This o-
ther answered and sayd thus. Sir I
am a deuyl of hel.but I am one of thē
that haue least power there. Al be yet
I haue power to make a womā to spe
ke,but and yf a woman begin oues to
speake,I noz al the deuyls in hel that
haue the moofte power be not able to
make a woman to be ftyll,noz to caufe
her to leue her speakyng.

C The end of this pleasant dialogue
declaryng the seueral properties of ÿ
two contrary disposers of the wyues
afozesayde.

C Impzynted at London in Paules
churche yearde, at the sygne of
the Sunne, by Antony
kytson.

¶ One dialogue, or

Colloquye of *Erasmus* (entituled *Diuersoria*) Translated oute of Latten into Englyshe: And
Imprinted, to the ende that the Iudgemét
of the Learned maye be hadde
before the Translator pro-
cede in therest.
By E. H.

¶ Imprinted at London in Fleetstreete, at the
signe of the Faucon by william Grif-
fyth, and are to be solde at his shop
in S. Dunstons Churchyard
in the west.
1556

¶ The Translatoꝛ to the
indifferent reader.

IF I were thꝛoughlye perſwaded
(gētle reader) ꝩ mine attempt of the
learned were in all points allowed
and the oꝛder in my tranſlation coꝛ-
reſpondent thereunto, I woulde at
this pꝛeſent pꝛoceede in mine enterpꝛiſe, with entent by gods helpe to finiſhe the tranſlation of
the whole boke: But becauſe I am vnlearned ⁊
therfoꝛe muſt not be mine owne iudge therein, I
geue the here a taſt of my ſtoꝛe foꝛ pꝛoofe of mine
abilitie: deſiring the at the leaſt wiſe not to be
offended at the ſame ſo boldly attem-
ted and ſimplye perfourmed.
Foꝛ ſithe mine entent is
good, ⁊ my good
wil not ſmall
I dare
at this pꝛeſent yelde
it to thy cutte-
ſye. Fare
wel.

¶ Thine in will (though not in
power)   E.H.

❧The speakers.

ʃ*Bertulphe.* *William.*

Hy haue men taken suche pleaʃure
and felicity(I pray you)in tariynge
it. or tʃi. dayes at Lions together,
when they trauaile through the con
trey:if I fall to trauailinge once, be
fore suche time as I be come vnto my iourneyes
ende,me thinks I am neuer at quiet in my mind.

William.

❧ Say ye ʃo in deede: And I put you out of
doubt, I wonder howe men can bee withdrawen
thence againe after they be once come thether.

Bertulphe.

❧ yea doe: And how ʃo I pray you:

William.

Mary ʃir becauʃe that is the verye place from
whence Vliʃʃes companions coulde in no wiʃe be
gotten by perʃwaʃion. There are the ʃweet Mer-
maides (that are ʃpoken of) I warrant ye. Aʃʃu-
redlie, no man is better bʃed at home at his own
houʃe then a gueʃt is entertained there in a common Inne.

Bertulphe.

Why: what is their order and bʃage there:

William.

Some woman or other did alwayes attende
vpon the table to chere the company with plea-
ʃaunt talke and prety conceites. And I tell you
the woinen are meruailous bewtiful and wel fauoured there. Firʃte of all the good wiʃe of the
houʃe came & welcomed bs,praying bs all there

B.i.   to

287

to bee merye, and to take well in woozthe suche pooze cheere as shee hadde prouided : when shee was gone,in commeth her Daughter (beeinge a verye propec woman) and tooke her roome: also whose behauioure and tongue were so pleasaunt and delectable, that she was able to make euen the grimme Sire Cato to bee merye and laugh, and besyde that they doe not talke wyth theyr guestes as with men whome they neuer sawe befoze, but euen so famplyatlye and freendlye, as if they were menne that were of their olde acquaintaunce.

Wertulphe.

℃ yea, thys is the ciuilytye of Fraunce in deede.

William.

℄And because the Mother and the Daughter coulde not bee alwayes in the waye (foz that they muste goe aboute theyr houssholde businesse, and welcome their other guestes in other places)a pzetye little minton Girle stode foz the there by and by (hauinge learned her liripuppe and lesson alreadye in all pointes I warraunte you)to make all the pastime that mighte be possible,and to aunswere (at omnia quare) all such as shoulde be busye to talke and dally with her, So shee didde pzolonge oz vpholde the Enterlude, till the goodwifes Daughter came vnto vs againe.Foz as foz the mother she was somewhat striken in yeres.

Her

Bertulphe.

℟ yea but tell vs what good cheere yee had there (I praye you) for a manne cannot fill his bellye with pleasaunte talke you knowe well inoughe,

William.

℟ I promise you faithfullye wee had notable good chere there, in so much that I wonder how they can entertaine their guestes so good cheape as they doe. And then when our table was takē vp, they fedde oure mindes wyth their merye deuises, leaste wee shoulde thinke the time wery lome. Me thought I was euen at home at mine owne house, and not a trauayler abroade in a straunge coūtry.

Bertulphe.

And what was the facion in your bed chambers there?

William.

℟ why e some wenches went in euerye corner giggelinge there, playing the wantons, and dalying with vs, of their owne motion they would aske whether we had any foule gere to washe or no. That they washed and brought vs cleane againe, what should I make a longe prcess or circumstance, we sawe nothinge els there but wenches and wemen sauinge in the stable. And yet

B.ii.

many

289

many times they would fetche theit bagaries in
thether also. When the guestes be going awaye,
they embrace them, and take their leaue sweetlye
with suche kindnes and curtesye , as if they were
all brethern, or (at least) nighe a kinne the one to
the other.

Bertulphe.

This behauiour doth well beseme Frenchmen
peraduenture, how be it the fashions of Duche
lande shall go for my monye when all is done,
which are altogether manlike.

William.

yt was neuer my chaunce to see the Contreye
yet: and therfore I pray you take so muche paine
as to tell in what sorte they entertaine a straunger with them.

Bertulphe.

I am not sure whether it be so in euerye place
or no, but I will not sticke to reherse that whiche
I haue sene with mine owne eyes. There no man
biddeth him welcome that comes, lest they shuld
seme to go about to procure a guest. And that of
all sauces, they accompt a dishonest and beggar
ly thing, and vnmete for their Demurenes & gra-
uitie. After you haue stoode crijnge oute at the
doore a good while, at the length some one or o-
ther peereth out his hed at the stoue window like
as a snaile should pepe out of his shell : for they
liue ther in stoues, til the somer be almoste in the
Tropick of Cancer. Then must you aske of him,
whether you may haue a lodging there or no: yf
be

he do not geue a contrary beck with his hed, you
may perceiue, that you shall haue entertainment
¶To those whiche aske where aboutes the stable
standes, he pointes vnto it with the wagging of
his hand . ¶There maye you vse youre horse after
your own diet , for no seruaunt of the house shall
once lay handes vnto it to help you. But if it bee
an Inne some what occupied or haunted , thē the
seruaunt sheweth there which is the stable, & tel=
leth you also a place where your horse shal stād,
full vnhansomely for that purpose god knoweth
for they reserue the better romes for the after com
mers, specially for the noble men , yf you finde a=
ny fault with any thinge, by an by they snub you
with this : Sir, if mine Inne please you not, goe
seeke an other elsewhere in the name of god in ci=
ties,it is longe ere they wil bring you hay forthe
for your horse, and when they do bring it,it is af=
ter a niuer facion I warraunt you , and yet will
they aske asmuch mony of you for it(in a maner)
as if it were Otes. After your horse is once dres=
sed you come with all your cariage into the stoue
with Bootes, Male,or Packe, and with Dirte,
Bag and Baggage and all . Euery man is vsed
to this generally.

William.

In Fraunce they haue certaine chaumbers for
the nonce, where guests may put of their clothes
may wipe or make clean thē selues , may warme
them selues: yea may take their ease to,if they bee
so disposed.

B.ii.   Bet

Bertulphe.

❡ yea, but here is no suche fa𝔠ions I tel you In the stoue, you pul of youre Bootes, you pull on youre Shooes, you chaunge youre Shirt it you bee so minded, you hange vp youre clothes all weate, with raine harde by the Chimney, and to make youre selfe d𝔷ye doe 𝔦lande by the same youre selfe, you haue also water sette readye fo𝔷 pour handes, which mo𝔰te commonly is so 𝔠leu= lye, that you mu𝔰te after seeke other water, to wa𝔰h꞉ of that water againe.

William.

❡ I commende them as menne not co𝔷rupted with to much fineue𝔰𝔰e o𝔷 daintine𝔰𝔰e.

Bertulphe.

❡ Thoughe it be youre chaunce to come the= ther aboute iiii. of the clocke at afternoone, yet 𝔰hall you not go to supper fo𝔷 all that vntill it be nine of the clocke at night, and sometime not be= fo𝔷e tenne.

William.

❡ How so=

Bertulphe.

❡ They make nothinge ready til they see all their gue𝔰tes come in, that they may serue them all vnder one without more adoe.

William.

❡ The𝔰e men seeke the neere𝔰t way to woo𝔷ke, I see wel.

Bertulphe.

you say true in deede: They doe so, and ther= fo𝔷e

foze often times there come all into one Stooue, lxxx. oz rC. Footemen, Hozsemen, Marchaunt= men, Mariners, Carters, Plowemen, Childzen, Wemen, hole and sicke.

William.

C Marye this is a communitye of lyfe in deede.

Bertulphe.

C One kembes his head there. In other doth rubbe of his sweat there. In other maketh cleane his startops oz bootes there. In other belcks out hys Garlicke there. What needis manye woz= des? There is as muche mingle mangle of par= sons there, as was in the old time at the Towze of Babell. And if they chaunce to see a straun= ger amonge them, whiche in his apparell semeth somewhat bzaue, galaunt and gentlemanlike, they all stand pzying vpon him with their eyes, gasing and gapinge as if some straunge beaste were bzought them out of Aphzick, in so much as after they are once set, they be eye him stil an end and neuer looke of, as men fozgetting thē selues that they be now at supper.

William.

At Rome, at Parise, and at Venice, no mā ma= keth any such wonderment at all.

Bertulphe.

Nowe it is a soze matter I tell you to call foz ought there al this while: when it is farre night and they looke foz no moze guestes at that time, then commeth fozthe an olde stager of the house, with

with a gray beard,a polled hed,a frowning coũ-
tenaunce,clad in il fauored apparaile,

William.

Yea mary suche fellowes as these you speak of,
should fill the Cardinals cups at Rome.

Bertulphe.

¶ He casting his eyes about,reckeneth vnto
him selfe howe manye therebe in the stoue at all,
the moe he seeth there, the greater he maketh his
fire,though the sonne beside doth greatly annoy
with his perching heat. Among them, this is ac-
coumpted the principallest pointe of good entertainment,if they all sweat like Bulles, that they
doe euen drop again. But if one not vsed to this
choking and smotheringe ayre , should chaunce
to open but a chinke of the window to keepe him
self from stifeling, he should by and by haue this
saied vnto him:Shut it I pray you, if you aunswere that you canne not abide it,ye haue this in
your nose for your labor,why:then go seeke you
an other Inne,on gods name.

William.

But me thinkes there can be no greater daunger for health,then that so many should drawe in
and out all one vapour:specially when the body
is in a sweat,and in this same place to eat meate
together , and to tarye together a great while in
company,for now I wil not speak of belchinges
that sauour of garlicks,nor offistinge,or fisteling
nor of stinking breths, many there be(I tel you)
that haue pokuy diseases, and euery desease hath
his

his proper infection. And surely the moste of them
haue the spanishe scabbe, oz as some terme it the
frenche pockes: thoughe now adaies one nation
hathe it commonlye asmuche as an other. I sup=
pose (I tel you) that there is as great ieobardye
in companyinge with these as it is with lepers,
and nowe gisse you howe muche difference is be=
twene this and the pestilence.

Bertulphe.

☞ Tushe man they bee stoute fellowes: they
doe scorne theise thinges, and make as it were
no accompt of them.

William.

But yet they are stout with hazardinge of ma=
ny a mannes helth I tell you plainely.

Bertulphe.

❡ Why: What should a man do? They haue
thus vsed them selues euer moze, and it is a to=
ken of constancy and stabilitie neuer to varye oz
geue ouer that whiche they haue once taken in
hand.

William.

But aboue twentye yeeres agone, there was
nothinge moze vsed amonge the Brabanders,
then the common Bathes. And now adaies, the
same are laied a side euery where: foz this straug
scabbe (I speake of) hathe taught men to come
no moze thether.

Bertulphe.

But go toe: Harken to the rest of my tale that
is behind. That grim bearded Ganimede coms

to vs afterwardes againe, and layeth as many
tables as he then thinkes will serue for the nom=
ber of his guestes, But Lord, what baggage
are the table clothes :if you saw them I dare say
you would think them hepen cloths, that are ta=
ken from the sailes of ships:they be so course, for
he hath apointed that viii. guests shall sit at one
table at the least. Nowe those that are acquain=
ted with the facion of the country, doe sit downe
euery man, where he listeth him selfe, for there is
no diuersitie or cursye I tell you there, betweene
the poore man and the riche, betweene the Mas=
ter and his seruaunt. They are all one. One as
good as an other, there is heere(as they say)no
difference betwene the shepherd and his dog.

William.

yea marye : this is the olde facion when all is
done,that Tiranny hath now abolished and put
away from amõg vs: I think Christ liued iump
after this maner on the earth when he was here
conuersaunt with his Apostles.

Bertulphe.

After they be all set,in commeth the frowning
minion againe, and once more falleth to recken
what company he hathe there: by and by retour=
ning he layeth euery one a trenchar, and a spone
of the same siluer : and then after that,hee setteth
downe a drinkinge glasse and within a whyle
brings

bisnges in bread which euery manne (at leysure)
chippeth and pareth for him selfe, whiles the po=
tage is a sethinge. They sit mopinge after thys
manner, otherwhiles a whole houre together,
ere they can get any thinge to eate.

William.

Why? Doe none of the guestes call earnest=
lye vpon them to haue in the Supper all this
while?

Bertulphe.

No, none of them all that knowes the
facion of the countrye. At the laste they are ser=
ued with Wyne: but youe woulde wonder to see
what small geare it is, Scoole men or Sophis=
tets shoulde drinke none other by myne aduise,
because it is so thinne and tarte: how bee it if a
guest shoulde chaunce (beside his shotte) to of=
fer Monye to one, and desyre him to gette some
better Wyne thenne that some other where, be=
cause he lykes it not: they first make as though
they hearde him not: but yet they bee eye hym
with suche a bigge an frowning countenaunce
as if the Deuyl should loke ouer LINCOLN
(as they doe saye) If you will not linne callinge
vppon them, theme they make youe this aun=
swere. So many EARLES and MAR-
QUESES, haue lodged here in our house, &
C.ii.   yet

yet the time is yet to come, that euer they founde
any fault with our wine. And therefore if ye fan=
cy it not, get ye packing in the name of God, and
seeke an other Jnne where ye liste . For they ac=
compt great men and noble men for men onely
in their contrye J tell you, setting their armes a=
broade in euery corner of their house for a Shewe.
Now by this time they are serued with a soupe,
to alay and pacify their pore hongry and crook=
ling stomackes, well nigh loste for meat, hard at
the heeles of that comes forthe the dishes with
greate ceremonie, pompe or solemnitie . For the
firste course they haue soppes or slices of bread,
soaked in flesshe brothe, or if it be a fisshe daye, in
the brothe of pulce. Then nexte they haue an o=
ther brothe: and after that they are serued wyth
flesshe twise sod, or fisshe twise het. And yet, after
this, they haue potage once againe, immediatly
after, they haue some stiffer meate til suche time
as they would beinge well amended with them,
they set roste on the table, or sodde fresshe fisshe,
whiche a man can not all together misslike. But
when it comes to that once they make spare and
whip it away at a sodaine J warraunt you, they
facion out euery thinge in his dew time & place.
And as the players of Enterludes or comedies,
are wonte in their Scenes , to entermedle theyr
Chories , so doe these Duche men serue forthe to
their guests, Soppes and Potage enterchange
ably or by course. But they prouide that the lat=
ter inde of the feast be best furnisshed.

Wel=

William.

And this (I tell you) is the poynte of a good Poet.

Bertulphe.

Besides this it were a sore offence for one all this while to say: Away with this dishe, no man doth eat of it, here you must sit out your time appointed, being so euen and iumpe, that I thinke they measure it oute by some water clockes . At length that bearded Grimson comes forth againe or els the Inholder him selfe; litle or nothing differing from his seruauntes in his apparaile and brauery. He asketh what cheere is with vs: by ¶ by some stronger wine is brought, and they caste a great loue to him that drinketh lustely : wheras he payes no more money that drinketh moste then he, that drinketh least,

William.

I put you out of doubt, it is a wonderful nature of the countrey.

Bertulphe.

yea, this doe they in deede: whereas there bee sometime there, that drink two times somuche in wine, as they paye in all for the shot. But before I doe make an end of this Supper, it is a wonderful thing to tell what noise and iangeling of tongues there is, after they begin all to bee well whitled with wine. what shoulde I neede manye wordes? All things there haue lost their hearing and are becom deafe. And many times disgused patches or corecomes doe come amonge them to

C.iii.   make

299

make sporte: whiche kinde of men, althoughe
of all other it be most to be abhorred, yet you wil
scant beleue howe muche the Germaines are de=
lighted with them. They keepe like a coile with
their singinge, theire chatting, their hoopinge
and hallowinge, theire praunsinge, theire boun=
singe, that the Stooue seemeth as if it woulde
fall downe vpon their heds, and none can heare
what an other saith. And yet all thys while they,
perswade them selues, that they liue as mannes
hearte canne thinke, or, as the day is broad and
longe to.

William.

Cwel nowe make an ende of this Supper,
I pray: for I am weary of so tedious a Supper
my selfe to.

Bertulphe.

CSo I will, At the laste when the cheese is
ones taken vp, whiche scantly pleaseth their ap=
tite, onlesse it craule ful of magots, that old Si=
nicore comes forth againe, bringinge with hym
a meate Trenchoure in his hande, vppon the
whiche with chalke he hath made certaine run=
delles and halfe rundelles: that same he layeth
downe vpon the table, loking very demurelye &
sadlye all the while. They that are acquainted
with those markes or skoares, doe laye downe
their monye, after them an other, then another,
vntill suche time as the trenchoure bee couered,
then

300

then markinge those whiche layed downe anye
thinge, he counteth or maketh reckening softely
vnto him selfe: if he misse nothing of that which
the reckeninge comes to, bee maketh a becke or
dieugard with his hed.

William.

℘ What if theer be any ouerplus there?

Bertulphe.

℘ Peraduenture he woulde glue it them a-
gaine, and some whiles they doe so, if it strike in
their braines.

William.

℘ And is there none that speaketh againste
this vnegall reckening?

Bertulphe.

℘ No, none that hathe any witte in his head,
for by and by they woulde saye thus vnto hym.
What kinde of man arte thou? I tell thee thou
thou shalt paye no more for thy Supper heere,
then other men do.

William.

℘ Marye this kinde of people is franke and
free I see wel.

Bertulphe.

℘ But if one (beeinge werye with trauaile)
should desire to go to bed as soone as Supper
is done, they will him tarye, till all the other go
to bed to.

William.

℘ Me thinkes I se Platoes common welth
heere.

Ber=

301

Bertulphe.

Then euerye mannes Cabin is shewed him, & in deede, nothinge elles but a bare chaumber for all that is there, is but beddes, and the Deuill a whit there is else beside there, eyther to occupye or els to steale.

William,

There is neatnesse or clenlinesse I warraunt you.

Bertulphe.

yea by roode, euen suche as was at the Supper. The Sheetes peraduenture were washed halfe a yeere before.

William.

And how fayres your horses all this while.

Bertulphe.

They are vsed after the same rate that the mē bee.

William.

But is this maner of entertainement in euery place there?

Bertulphe.

In some place it is more curteous, in some place againe, it is more currishe then I haue made rehersall, howbeit generalipe it is euen after this order.

William.

What would you say if I should now tell you how strangers are entreated in that part of Italy which they call Lōbardy, and again in spaine howe they be vsed, and how in Englande and in Wales for Englishe men in conditions are halfe Frenche

Frenche, halfe Dutche as men indifferente betweene both. Of theise two contries, Welche men say that they are the right Brittaines first inhabiting the land.

Bertulphe.

℃ Mary I pray thee hartely tell me, for it was neuer my fortune to trauaile into them.

William.

℃ Nay, I haue no layture nowe at this time, for the Mariner bad me bee with him at three of the clock, except I would be left behinde, and he hath a Packette of mine. Another time wee shall haue layture enough to tell of these thinges our bellies full.

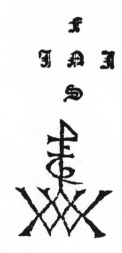

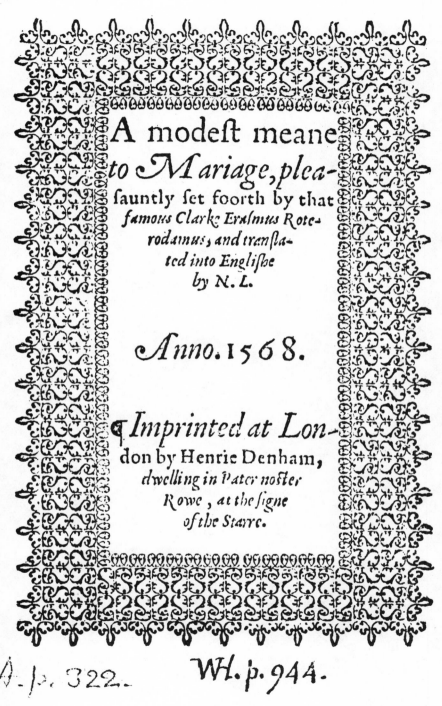

A modeſt meane
to *Mariage,* plea-
ſauntly ſet foorth by that
famous Clarke Eraſmus Rote-
rodamus, and tranſla-
ted into Engliſhe
by N. L.

Anno. 1568.

¶*Imprinted at Lon-*
don by Henrie Denham,
dwelling in Pater noſter
Rowe , at the ſigne
of the Starre.

¶To the right worship-
full Maister Francis Rogers
Esquire, one of the Gentlemen pen-
sioners vnto the Queenes Maiestie, Nicholas Leigh wisheth long & quiet
lyfe, with much increase
of vertue and
worship.

HEN I REMEM-
ber (gentle Maister Ro-
gers) the auncient ac-
quaintance and friend-
ship, and the daylie and
accustomed metings, re-
course and familiaritie
that (amōg the rest) did
happen and passe betwene vs in times past, in those
our yong and tender yeares; and in those famous
places of studie, vnto the which we were by oure
friendes appointed and then sent for learning sake.
And when moreouer, I doe remember, waye, and
cōsider therin on the one side, that state and condition of life, in the which I was then, with that,
which for my part on the other side, I doe now find
and haue long since felt and tasted of, I cannot but
recken and thinke that time most happily passed
                    A.ij.   which

307

The Epistle

which I bestowed in the trauaile and study of good
letters. For besides the inestimable fruit, & the in-
comparable pleasure & delectation, that the Muses doe bring vnto the studious, beside the sweete
rest of minde, voyde of all worldly cares and troubles, the faire & pleasaunt walkes, which we there
(with a number of vertuous, and well disposed,
and a sort of learned, ciuili, friendly and faithfull companions) enioyed, togither with the wholesome and cleane diet, not infected with outragious
or any surfetings (a vice else where to much vsed)
what honest and godly exercises had we then there
to the furtherance and increase of vertue, & to the
abandoning of vice? insomuch that in a maner it
hath fared with me euer since my departing thēce,
as with one that being expelled and exuled from a
second Paradise, replenished and adorned with all
kinde of flagrant & of most wholesome and sweete
flowers and delights, is presently fallen as it were
into a darke & an yrkesome thicket of bushes and
brambles of the cares and troubles of this worlde,
daylie readie, not onely to molest and perturbe the
quiet studious minde, but also so complete with an
infinite number of displeasures, dammages, and
daungers on euerye side that (verye much according to the auncient and wonted prouerbe) I may
now iustly say vix fugiet Scyllam, qui vult
vitare

The Epistle

vitare Charybdim. *Wherefore that mans saying seemed not altogither voyde of reason, that sayde, that if there were anye choyse to be had as touching the estate of man, the better parte and the first thereof was not to be borne at al, the next vnto that was to die verie shortly. And yet by the way neuerthelesse, as he that hath bene once in any suche kinde of Paradise or place of pleasure, as is aforesaide, hath alwayes nowe and then some motions and occasions, to cast his sorrowfull eye with a mournfull minde towardes the same: euen so I of late beholding and lamenting that chaunged place and state of life, and in the meane season peruusing some pieces of mine olde exercises which I had then and did there (whereof I was alwayes bolde partly to make you priuie, as one among all others whose discreete iudgement and towardnesse in learning togither with the great curtesie and singuler humanitie and friendship, and the passing readie and great pleasantnesse of wit, ioyned therewith was then certes not a little had in admiration and embraced euery where) happily I founde certaine loose papers of two Dialogues of the famous and excellent Clarke* Erasmus of Roterodame, *by me translated into englishe (partly for the pleasantnesse of the matter, as it seemed vnto me then, partly alsa for the*

A.iij.   proofe

proofe and triall of my selfe what I coulde doe in translating, and lastly as the matter semed swete and pleasaunt, so not altogither voide of godlye and wholesome exhortations and lessons, for all sortes no lesse necessarie than profitable. Which when I had with earnest view pervsed, and hauing in minde diuers times to gratifie your goodnesse with some friendly token of remembraunce, forthwith I thought (renuing my woted exercises) to dedicate these two Dialogues vnto you. Whose knowledge and learning I know, and gentlenesse therwithal to be such, that I am in an assured hope that (vntill I may giue better) ye will vouchsafe in the meane season thankefully to accept these my recreations, and these few lines at my handes as a pledge and a poore present of the continuall remembraunce, and the vnfeyned good will I beare towards you, & your vertuous demerites. Wherin notwithstanding, albeit peraduenture the exercise of study and learning, and especially the matter it selfe therein contained maye seeme to bee of very small importance or pleasure, & rather otherwise different or something disagreeable vnto your vocation on euerie side, and also vnto all such for the most part as in the roome and place of armes, are called towardes the seruice of the Princes Maiestie, and of their Countrie (Rara enim

The Epistle

enim inter Arma & literas vel togas est
amicitia vel, societas) *Yet I knowing the
great reuerence and the singular regard and estimation that you do beare, and alwayes haue borne
towardes the learned and towardes good letters,
for the pleasant and fruitefull knowledge that you
your selfe haue most happily and with great dex-
teritie both reaped and tasted among them in
times past, I doubt not but that (waying the wor-
thinesse of the Author of them, and accepting the
faithfull indeuours of me the rude translator of
them) you will be content to permit the same to
passe vnder your wing , and so much (I know) the
rather for that they both doe tende to vertues purpose. The one of them being betweene a Woer and
his Feere, wherein albeit the naturall ouerthwart-
nesse of the womanishe minde, doth now and then
burst out as out of the frayler and weaker vessell,
yet is therein a godlye kinde of woeing without
any scurilitie, very pleasantly, liuely, and plainly
declared and set forth, to the good behauiour and
honest inducement and furtherance of such as are
yet to take that matter or enterprise in hand, farre
from prouoking any vice, as the maner and guise
of a number of lasciuious Louers and fayned
woers nowe a dayes is, whose craftie and counterfet dealings, fonde iestures and motions, and vn-*
A.iiij.　　comely

The Epistle

comely and vaine communications and ydle talks
is better to be passed ouer with silence than paper
to be stained therewith, or any time to bee spent
therein. The other is betweene a yong man and a
light Woman, who in times past had bene further acquainted then honestie required, and hee
hauing bene absent fram hir for a certaine space,
at last repaired to hir house, who after hir accustomed maner and wont, beganne to entise
and allure him to their former follies, who percey-
uing hir purpose therein, discreetly and properly
perswaded hir by diuers and sundrie godly and
vertuous reasons to leaue and forsake that kinde
of life, as of all other most detestable, and in the
ende making hir thereby to loath hir frayle and
accustomed follies, bringeth hir vnto an honest
and chaste conuersation. Thus the effect of the
whole matter you haue in few words. Accept therfore (I praye you) this my simple doing in good
part, weying my good will in the friendly Ballance
of your accustomed gentlenesse, which I trust shall
somewhat counterpaise the vnworthinesse of
this my so grosse and rude a translation of so worthy a writer.
Vale.

**Yours vnfeynedly Ni-
cholas Leigh.**

To the Reader.

I HAVE (GENTLE Reader) set foorth to thy viewe, two Dialogues of the Reuerende & renowmed Clarke *Erasmus Roterodamus* : whose learning, vertue, and authoritie is of sufficient force to defend his doyngs. But bicause I haue chaunged his eloquent stile, into our English phrase : and thereby altered his liuerie, and embased the perfite grace of his Muse, I am compelled to craue pardon of this my doings, consider I beseeche thee (learned Reader) that if it had still rested in that Noble language wherein hee left it, although thy knowledge had yelded thee greater felicitie than this my trauaile can, yet thousandes, which by this mine indeuour may draw out some sweete sap of these his pleasant and fruitfull doings, might(thorow ignorance)haue wanted thys peece of delyght. Therfore the offence (if any be)is made to *Erasmus* a mã of that pacience in his lyfe, as I assure
my

The Preface

my self that this my bold dealing with
him, can not a whit disquiet his ghost.
Harme to thee at all it can not bee, for
that I haue not digressed from mine
Author. Pleasant and profitable I hope
it will be to many of my country folks
whose increase in vertue I greatlye desire. Then suffer mee I pray thee to rest
with thy quiet and thankfull iudgement: whereby thou shalt vrge me to
attempt farther enterprise (perchance
to thy delight.) Thus assuring my selfe
of thy lawfull fauour, I rest voyde of
care of the vnlearneds reproche, if they
beyonde their skill shall couet to
chat. And wishing to thee thy
full delight in learning &
to them increase of
knoweledge , I
bid you both
farewel.

FINIS.

Pamphilus, the Louer,
Maria, the woman
beloued.

GOod morrowe cruell, good morow ruthlesse, good morow (I say) thou stony harted woman. Maria. I wishe you the same againe *Pamphilus* as often, and as muche as you please. And by what name you lyke best to be saluted. But in the meane while it seemeth you haue forgotten my name, my name is *Maria*. Pamphilus. It might more rightlye haue bene *Martia*. Maria. And why so I beseech you ? what haue I to doe with *Mars* ? Pamphilus : For as that God counteth it but a pastime to murther and kill men, euen so doe you. Herein yet more cruell then *Mars*, for you murther him that hartily loueth you. Maria. God wordes I praye you, where is that heape of deade bodies whom I haue murthered ? where is the bloud of them which by me are slaine ? Pamphilus. One life-lesse bodye thou seest present wyth thine eyes,

eyes, if (pardie) thou sæst me. Ma. What saye you man ? doe you both talke and walke, and yet dead ? I pray to God I neuer mæte with ghostes moꝛe to be feared. Pam. Thus thou makest but a laughing matter of it. Nathelesse thou hast reft me wofull creature my life, and moꝛe cruelly doest murther me, than if thou should stab me into the body with a weapon, foꝛ now am I miserably toꝛne and vexed with long toꝛments. Maria. Yea god Loꝛd ? tell mæ how manye women with childe haue lost their fruite by mæting with you ? Pam. Yet this pale wanne colour sheweth mæ to bæ moꝛe bloudlesse than any shadowe. Ma. But this palenesse (thanked be God) is died with some Uiolet colour, you are euen so pale as a Chery waxing ripe, oꝛ a Grape when he commeth to his purple skin. Pam. Thus with disdaine ynough you mocke a man in state rather to be pittied. Ma. Why in case you belæue not mæ, take the Glasse, & belæue your owne eyes. Pam. I woulde wishe no better Glasse, neyther (I suppose) is there anye, moꝛe clære, than that in which I pꝛesentlye

lye behold my selfe euen now. Ma. What Glasse speake you off? Pam. Marie euen your owne eyes. Ma. Ouertharter: how thou talkest alwayes lyke thy selfe, but howe proue you your selfe to bee deade? Doe ghostes & shadowes vse to eat meat? Pam. They doe, but find no sauour therin, no more doe I. Ma. And what, what doe they eate I praye? Pam. Mallowes, Leekes and Lupines. Ma. But you (I hope) let not to eate Capons and Partriches. Pam. I graunt, howbeit I feele no more pleasure in eating them, than if I should crashe vpon Mallowes, or Beetes, without Pepper, wine and vinegar. Ma. Alack for you good man, and yet you are in meetely good lyking, & do ghostes speake also? Pam. Euen as I doe with a verye pewling and faint voice. Ma. But not long since, when I hearde you checking with mine other suter, your voice was not very feeble pardie. Moreouer I beseech you tell me this, doe ghostes vse to walke? are they clad in garments? doe they eftsoones sleepe? Pam. Yea more than all that, they practise the acte of kinde, but after

their

their owne maner. Ma. Now by the faith of my bodye you are a pleasaunt trifler. Pam. But what will you saye, if I proue this by substantiall and strong reasons (I meane) my selfe to be dead, and you to be a murtherer? Ma. God shylde that(friend *Pamphile*) but let me heare your Sophi-strie. Pam. First you wil graunt me this? (I suppose) that death is naught else but a seperation of the soule from the body. Ma. I graunt. Pamphilus. But graunt it so ý you reuoke and call it not back againe, af-terwarde. Ma. No more I wyll. Pam. Secondly, you wil not denie but he which reaueth the soule, wherein consisteth life, is a murtherer. Ma. I consent. Pam. You will I am sure graunt me this lykewyse, which most graue and credible Authors haue affirmed, & by the consent and iudge-ment of all ages hath bene holden truth and allowed, (I meane) that the soule of a man is not where he liueth, but where he loueth. Ma. You must vtter that after a more grosse, and plaine sorte, for in good faith I perceyue not your meaning. Pam. And I am the more sorie, and euill at ease, **bicause**

Dialogues.

bicause you doe not perceiue and fœle this
to be true, as well as I doe. Ma. Make
me to fœle it then. Pam. As well mightest
thou bid me, make an Adamant fœle it.
Ma. Now truely I am a yong wench, not
a stone. Pam. Truth, but moze harde yet
than the Adamant stone. Ma. But pzo-
cœde with your argument. Pam. Those
which are rapt in the spirite, oz fallen into a traunce (as they call it) neyther heare,
noz sée, noz smell, noz fœle any thing, no
though you would kil them. Ma. Surely I
haue hard say so. Pa. And what think you
to be the cause of this insensibilitie. Ma. I
would learne that of you which are a Philosopher. Pam. Bicause (pardie) the soule
oz minde is in heauen, where it hath that
which it behemently loueth, & is not pzesent with the body. Ma. And what is next?
what conclude you vpon this? Pam. As-
kest thou what O cruell? euen this neces-
sarily followeth, my selfe to be deade, and
thy selfe to bée a murtherer. Ma. Why,
where is your soule become and God wil?
Pam. There it is, where it loueth. Ma.
And who hath reft it from you? why sigh
you

you man: speake and feare not, you shall not be hindered by me. Pam. A certaine cruell and pittilesse mayde, whome neuerthelesse I cannot finde in my hart to hate, being by hir spoyled of my life. Ma. Ah, a louing hart, ah gentle nature. But why do you not againe take from hir, hir soule, and serue hir as they saye, with the same sause. Pam. The happiest in the worlde, were I, if I could make that exchaunge (I meane) that hir minde might come dwell in my brest, in sorte as mine hath wholye dwelled in hir body. Ma. But wil you giue me leaue now eftsones a while to play the Sophister his part with you: Pam. Nay the Sophistresse parte. Ma. Is it possible that one and the same bodie both haue the soule and be without the soule. Pam. Not both togither or at one time. Ma. When the soule is awaye, then the body (you say) is deade. Pam. Truth. Ma. And it lyueth not but when the soule is present withall: Pam. Be it so verily. Ma. How commeth this to passe then, that the soule being there where it loueth, the body yet wherout it is departed, neuerthelesse lyueth: for if it ly-

ueth

tieth in one place, when it loueth in an other, by what reaſō is it called *Exanime Corpus*, as you would ſay, a lifeleſſe body, ſince it hath life and ſenſe in it. Pam. By ſaint Marie you playe the Sophiſtres moetelyé well, howbeit you cannot ſnarle me in ſuch chicken bandes. That ſoule which after a ſort gouerneth the bodye of a liuing creature being in ſuche caſe is improperly called the ſoule, for in very dede it is a certaine ſmall portion of the ſoule, which remaineth behind, euen as the ſauor of Roſes tarieth ſtill in the hande of him, which bare them, when ẏ very Roſes themſelues be done away. Ma. J ſee well inough it is hard to take a foxe in a pitch, but anſwere me to this alſo. Is not he a doer which murthereth. Pam. What elſe. Ma. And is not ẏ partie a ſufferer, who is murthered? Pam. Yes. Ma. How commeth it to paſſe then, that ſince he which loueth is the doer and ſhee which is beloued is but the ſufferer, ſhe ſhould be infamed for a murtherer, which is beloued. When as in verie dede, he that loueth rather murthereth himſelf? Pam. Nay, it is contrarie, for he that lo-

B.j.   ueth

ueth suffreth, she that is beloued doth. Ma.
That shall you neuer proue true with the
consent of our chiefe *Areopagites* of Gram-
mer. Pam. But this will I proue true by
the consent of the whole Parliament of
Logitians. Ma. But aunswere me to this
againe, loue you with your wil, or against
your wyll? Pam. With my will. Maria.
Ergo, sithence it is in frée choise to loue, or
not to loue, whoso loueth, is a murtherer
of himselfe, and wrongfullye accuseth the
pore wench beloued. Pam. Why? I say
not that the wench murthereth bicause she
is beloued, but bicause she loueth not a-
gaine the party which loueth hir: for (truth
it is) she is guilty of murther, which might
saue a mans life and will not. Ma. I put
case a yong man cast his loue vpon one,
which he ought not to loue, or maye not
lawfully obtaine, as an other man hys
wyfe, or a Virgine, which hath professed
continuall chastitie, shall she loue him a-
gaine, so to preserue and saue hir louer?
Pam. But this yong man loueth that,
which to loue. is both lawfull and godly,
and standeth both with reason and equity,
and

Dialogues.

and yet neuerthelesse is cast away. That in case you set light by the criime of homicide, I will aguilt you also of sorcerie and enchaunting me. Ma. Marrie gods forbod man, what will you make of me a *Circes* ymp̃e, a witch? Pa. Pea and somewhat more cruell yet, than euer was *Circes*. For I had rather be a groueling Hog or beare, then as I am, without life or soule. Ma. And with what kinde of sorcerie I praye ye doe I destroy men. Pam. By euill aspect. Ma. Will you then that I hurt you no more with loking vpon you? Pam. Not so for Gods sake, but rather loke more vpon me. Ma. If mine eyes be witches, how hapneth it then that other also do not consume awaye, whome I loke vpon as ofte as you, therfore I feare me much, ỹ bewitching is in your owne eyes, not in mine. Pam. Why thinke you it not inough to slea *Pamphilus*, except you triumph ouer him being dead. Maria. Oh queint handsome, nise dead body: when shall your funerals be prouided for. Pam. Sooner than you thinke ywisse, except you remedie in time. Ma. I remedie good Lord? am I

B.ij.   able

323

able to doe such a cure ? Pam. Pea surely: all were I deade, it lyeth in you to rayse me vp againe to life, and that with a light thing. Maria. As you say, peraduenture I might doe it, if some bodye woulde helpe me to the herbe *Panaces*, wherevnto they ascribe so great a vertue. Pam. There nædeth none herbes to doe it, only vouch-safe to loue againe, what is moꝛe easie to be perfourmed ? nay rather what is moꝛe due and iust ? otherwise you shall neuer acquite your selfe of manspilling. Maria. And befoꝛe what iudgement seate shall I be arrayned, befoꝛe the seuere Areopage-tes and God will ? Pam. Not so, but be-foꝛe the tribunall seate of *Venus*. Maria. Best of al, foꝛ they say she is a patient and pitiful Goddesse. Pam. Say you so, there is not one amongst them all, whose wꝛath is moꝛe to be feared. Ma. Why, hath she a thunderbolte? Pam. No. Maria. Hath she a thꝛæfoꝛked mase like *Neptune*? Pam. Not so. Ma. Hath she a speare as *Pallas*? Pam. Neyther: but shæ is a Goddesse of the Sea. Maria. I come not within hir kingdome. Pam. But she hath a boye.

Maria.

Dialogues.

Maria. I feare no boyes. Pam. He is readie to reuenge, and will paye home when
he striketh. Ma. And what shall he doe to
me? Pam. What shall he doe: the gods
fore let him. I will prognosticate none
euill vnto one, whome I beare good will.
Ma. Yet tell me I pray you, I will take
no conceit of it. Pam. Then will I tell
you if you shall disdaine this louer, who
doubtlesse is not vnworthie your loue, verily I beleue, that same boy(peraduenture
at the commaundement of his mother) wyll
thirle into your heart a launce embrued
with to bad a poyson,wherby you shal set
your affection miserably vppon some hob-
lout, who shall not loue you any whit a-
gaine. Ma. Marrie that were a plague in
déede,of all other most to be detested. Certes I had rather to die, than to be entang-
led in the loue of one which is deformed, &
could not finde in his hart to loue me likewise againe. Pam. But it is not long
time, since there was a right notable example of this euil,which I now speak off,
shewed in a certaine yong damzel.Ma.In
what place, and I may be so bold as to ask
B.iij.   you?

you? Pam. At the Citie *Aurelia*. Ma. Howe many yeares ago? Pam. Howe many yeares, nay, it is scarse yet ten monethes. Ma. And what was the Mayores name? whereat sticke you? Pam. Nothing. I knewe hir as well as I knewe you. Ma. Why tell you me not hir name then? Pam. Bicause I like not the lucke therof, I had rather she had had any other name: She had euen the verie name that you haue. Ma. Who was hir father? Pam. He is yet man aliue, and amongst the Lawyers is one of chiefe estimation, and of substantiall welth. Ma. Tell me his name also. Pam. *Mauritius*. Ma. His surname, Pam. His surname was *Aglaus*. Ma. Liueth the mother yet? Pam. She departed of late. Ma. Of what disease died shée? Pam. Of what disease, quoth you, for méere sorrow & heauinesse. And the father himselfe albeit he is a man of a strong nature scaped very narowly. Ma. And may I learne at your hand also the name of the mother. Pam. With all mine hart, who is he that knoweth not *Sophrona*. But what meane you by this
questio∫

questioning ? Thinke you that I contriue
fables for you. Ma. Why should I thinke
so , that is rather to be suspected in oure
kinde, but tell on, what befell vnto this
mayde . Pam. This damzell was come of
an honest stock (as I haue said) and wanted no welth to hir preferment : for bewty
and shape of body, also goodly to beholde,
what nædeth many words, she was well
worthy to haue lien by a Prince his side.
She had a wower, who earnestly besought
hir good will, a man for personage & bew-
tie not vnlike hir self. Ma. And what was
his name?Pam. Alas,God blesse me from
the luck, hys name also was *Pamphilus,*
when he had done all that he could,and as-
sayed all waies possible to obtaine hir good
will,she still obstinately despised him. In
fine, the yong man pined away with sorrow,and dyed.Not long after,this wench
beganne to dote vppon such a handsome
squire,as for his personage,I might more
rightly call an Ape than a mã.Ma. What
say you man ? Pam. She was so farre fallen in the brakes with him, that I am not
able to expresse. Ma. What, so proper a
B.iij. wench

wench with so vnsightly a péece? Pam.
He had a head made like a sugar lofe, the
heare thereof growing as it were by stit-
ches and that knotted, vnkempt, full of
scurfe and nittes, and a good parte of hys
scalpe was bared by the disease called *Alopecia*, his eies sunk into his head, his nose-
thrils wide & turning vpwardes, a mouth
like an Ouen with rotten téeth, and a
stamering tongue, a scuruy beard, a bunch
backe, a belly like a tode, and legges as
right as a paire of horse hames. Ma. Marry
sir you describe him to be a very *Thersites*?
Pam. Nay besides al this, they say, he had
but one of his eares. Ma. Peraduenture
he had lost the other in some battaile. Pa.
No surely, euen in peace. Ma. Who durst
be so bolde to doe that? Pam. Who but
Dionysius that cutteth of eares at the Pille-
ry. Ma. Wel, it may be yet y his substance
at home was such as made a full mendes
for all the deformitie that you haue spoken
of. Pam. Nay surely: he had vnthriftilye
spent all, and ought moze than bee was
worth, with this suchen an husbande doth
this so goodly a wench nowe lead hir life.
Ma.

Alopecia *is a disease that cau-seth the heare to fill off.*

Thersites *a Prince, that came with the Greekes to the siege of Troye, which in p rson and condi-cion was of all other most de-formed.*

328

Dialogues.

Ma. You haue declared a thing much to be pittied. Pam. Surely it is true, the Goddesse *Nemesis* woulde so haue it, that the iniurie of the yong man, whome shée despised might be requited of hir. Ma. I would rather wish to be destroyed with a thunderbolt out of hande, than to be yoked with such a mate. Pam. Therfore beware how you prouoke this Ladie, who reuengeth disdaine, and frame your harte to loue him againe, who loueth you. Ma. If that may suffice (loe) I loue you again. Pam. But I craue that loue at your hand, which should be perpetuall and to loue me as your owne. I séeke a wife, not a friend. Ma. I know that well inough, but that thing requireth long deliberation, and much aduisement, which when it is done, cannot be vndone againe. Pam. I haue deliberated vppon it to long for my part. Ma. Well (I réede you) take héede, least loue who is not the best counseller beguile you, for men say that loue is blinde. Pam. Nay, that loue hath eyes which springeth vpon iudgement : I doe not therfore take you to be such a one as you are, bicause I

Nemesis, the Goddesse of wrath or indignation.

Delibe-
randum
est diu,
quod sta-
tuendum
est semel.

loue

loue you ; but I loue you for that I plainly sée you to be such a one. Ma. Beware
I say, you mistake me not, you maye bée
ouerséene, if you had worne the shoe,
then you shoulde perceyue where it wrin-
geth. Pam. I must put it in a venture, although by many good tokens I conceyue a
hope of better lucke. Ma. Whye, are you
skilfull in signes and tokens, are you become an Augur? Pam. Yea marry am I.
Ma. By what Augurall signes I praye
you, do you coniecture that it shalbe thus?
hath the night Crowe taken hir flight before you? Pam. She flieth for fooles. Ma.
What, haue you séene a cowple of Doues
come flying towardes you on the right
hande? Pam. No such thing, but I haue
knowne for the space of certaine yeares
the verteous and honest behauiour of your
parents, that is a birde not least to be regarded (I think)to be come of a good stock.
Moreouer, I am not ignorant with what
wholesome instructions, and verteous er-
amples you haue bene traded and brought
vp by them. And truely good education is
of more effect than good Parentage. This
is

Augurs bee they which by certaine signes in birdes and beasts des-crie things to come.

is an other signe which moueth me to con=
ceyue a good hope, beside this, betwene my
parents, which I hope I neede not to be a=
shamed of and yours, haue (as I suppose)
bene, no smal loue and friendship. Yea we
our selues from our biggens (as they say)
haue bene brought vp togither, & not much
vnlike one vnto another in nature and dis=
position. Now our age, substance, estima=
tion, and bloude are as well betweene vs
two, as betweene both our parentes in a
maner equall. Lastly that which in friend=
ship is the chiefe thing, your maners see=
meth not the worste to square vnto my
minde and liking, for it maye bee that a
thing is simply and of it selfe right excel=
lent and yet not apt and meete for some
vse. How my maners frameth vnto your
minde againe I knowe not. These, these
be the birdes (my Ioy) which putteth mee
in an assured hope, that a coniunction
betweene vs two, shall be right ioyfull,
pleasant, stable, & sweete, so that you could
finde in your hart to sing that song, which
I so much desire to heare. Maria. What
song is that you woulde haue me to sing.
Pam.

Two pleasant

I am thine.
Be thou
mine.

Pam. I will teach you the tune thereof.
Sum tuus, say you againe, *Sum tua.* Ma.
The song in déede is short, but me thinks
it hath a verie long ende, and much matter
dependeth thereon. Pam. What forceth
it for the length, so it be pleasant & swéete
vnto you. Ma. I loue you so well that I
woulde not haue you doe that, wherof you
should herafter repent & beshrew your self.
Pa. I pray you neuer speake of any repen-
tance. Ma. Peraduenture you shoulde o-
therwise estéeme of me, when eyther age or
sicknesse shall chaunge this fourme or fauour. Pam. Why? this body of myne (O
my déere) shall not alwayes continue in
this estate, thus prest and lustie, but I respect not so muche this flourishing and
bewtifull house, as I doe him that dwelleth therein. Maria. What meane you by
that you speak of him that dwelleth within? Pam. Verily I meane your well disposed and vertuous minde, whose beawtie
alwayes encreaseth with age. Ma. What,
your sight is yet more pleasant than *Linx,*
if you can espie that, through so many co-
uerings. Pam. Yea certes with my mind

I

332

Dialogues.

I doe right well espie your minde : more
ouer (I saye) in those childꝛen which God
shall sende vs, wée shall as it were, ware
yong againe. Maria . But in the meane
time virginitie is lost. Pam . Truth, in
good faith, tell me if you had a goodly oꝛch
yarde plat, whether woulde you wish no
thing should therein grow but blossomes,
oꝛ else had you rather(the blossomes fallen
away) beholde your trées fraught and la
den with pleasaunt fruite ? Maria. Howe
sliely he reasoneth. Pam. At the least aun
swere me to this : whether is it a better
sight foꝛ a Uine to lye vppon the grounde
and rot, oꝛ the same to embꝛace a poale, oꝛ
an elme, and lode it full with purple gra
pes ? Maria. Now sir aunswere me to this
againe, whether is it a moꝛe pleasant sight
a Rose trim and milkewhite , yet grow
ing on his stalk, oꝛ the same plucked with
the hande , and by little and little withe
ring away ? Pam. Certes in mine opi
nion the rose is the happiest, and commeth
to the better ende, which withereth and di
eth in the hande of man, delighting in the
meane while both the eies and nosethꝛils,
than

than thother which withereth on the bush,
for there muste it nœdes wither also at
length, euen as that wine hath better luck
which is dzunken, than that which stan=
deth still, and is turned into vinigar. And
yet the flowzing beautie of a woman doth
not decay fozthwith as sœne as she is ma=
ried, foz I knowe some my selfe, who be=
foze they were maried, were pale colozed,
faint, and as it were pined away, who by
the friendly felowship of an husband, haue
wared so faire, and welfauoured,that you
would think they neuer came to the flow=
er of their beautie till then. Ma. But foz
all your saying, virginity is a thing much
beloued and lyked with all men. Pam . I
graunt you,a yong woman,a virgine,is a
fayze, ₰ gœdly thing,but what by course of
kind is moze bnsœmly thã an old wrink=
led maide:Had not your mother bene con=
tented to lose that flower of hir virginitie,
surely we had not had this flower of your
beautie . So that in case (as I hope) our
mariage be not barren,foz the losse of one
virgine we shall paye God manye. Ma.
But they saye chastitie is a thing wherein
God

Dialogues.

God is much delighted. Pam. And therefore doe I desire to couple my selfe in mariage with a chast mayden, that with hir I
may leade a chaste life. As for our mariage
it shall rather be a mariage of our minds,
than of our bodies, we shall increase vnto
Christ, we shall increase vnto the comon
welth. How little shall this matrimonie
differ frō virginitie? & peradventure hereafter we shall so liue togither, as blessed
Marie liued with Ioseph, no man cometh
at the first to perfection. Maria. What is
that I heard you say euen now, must virginity be violated and lost, therby to learn
chastitie? Pam. Whye not, euen as by
drinking of wine moderately, we learn by
little and little to forbeare wine vtterlye,
which of these two sœmeth vnto thœ to be
more temperat, he that sitting in the mids
of many daintie dishes, abstaineth from
them all, or he which forbeareth intempe-
rauncie, hauing none occasiō to moue him
vnto the same? Ma. I suppose him to haue
the more confirmed habite of temperance
whom plentie alwayes prest can not corrupt . Pam. Whether deserueth more
the

the prayse of chastitie, he that geldeth him selfe, or he which keping his members all and sounde abstaineth from all womans companie? Ma. Uerily by my consent the latter shal haue the praise of chastitie, that other of mad follie. Pam. Why? those which by vowe haue abiured matrimonye doe they not after a sort gelde themselues: Maria. Uerily it seemeth so. Pam. Thus you see, it is no vertue to forbeare womens companie. Maria. Is it no vertue? Pam. Marke me this, if it were simplye a vertue to forbeare the companie of a woman, then shoulde it be also a vice to vse the companie of a woman, but sometime it befalleth that it is sin to refuse the acte, and a vertue to vse it. Ma. In what case is it so? Pam. In case the husband requireth of his wife the debt of marriage, euen so often as he shall do it, especially if he requireth it for the desire of generation. Ma. But what if he be fleshfond and wanton, may she not lawfully denie it him? Pam. She maye admonish him of his fault and rather gently perswade him to bridle hys affections, to giue him a flat nay when he

fraineth

frayneth vpon hir, she may not. Albeit J
here verie felwe men complaine of their
wyfes vncurtesie this way. Ma. Yet mee
thinks libertie is swæte. Pam. Nay rather virginitie is a heauie burthen. J shall
be to you a King, and you shall be to me a
Quæne. And eyther of vs shall rule the
familie, as we thinke good, take you thys
to be a bondage ? Ma. The common sort
calleth mariage an halter. Pam. Now on
my fayth they are well worthie an halter
that so termeth it. Tell me J praye you
is not your soule bounde vnto your body?
Ma. J thinke so. Pa. Yea surely euen as
a bird vnto hir cage, & yet if ye should aske
him the question, whether he woulde bée
losed or no, J suppose he woulde saye nay.
And why so? bicause he is willinglie and
gladlie bounde therevnto. Ma. We haue
little to take to neither of vs both. Pam.
So much the lesse indaungered to fortune
are wee, that little you shall encrease at
home wyth sauing, which as they coun-
teruayleth a great reuenue, and J abroad
with diligence. Ma. An houshold of chil-
dren bringeth innumerable cares. Pam.

C.i. On

On the other side agayne, the same chil=
dren bringeth infinite pleasures; and of=
tentimes requiteth the parentes naturall
paines to the vttermost., with great ouer=
plusse. Ma. Then to lead a barren life in
marriage is a great miserie. Pam. Why
are you not now barraine? tell me whe=
ther had ye rather neuer be borne, or borne
to die. Ma. Certes I had rather be borne
to die. Pam. So that barrainnesse is yet
more miserable which neyther hadde, nor
shall haue child, euen as they be more hap=
pie which haue alreadie lyued; then they
which neuer haue, nor shall hereafter be
borne to liue. Ma. And what be those, I
praye you which neyther are, nor shall be.
Pam. For he that cannot finde in his hart
to suffer and abide the chaunges, & chaun=
ces, wherunto all we indifferently be sub=
iect; as well men of pore estate, as Kings,
& Emperours, he is not to dwell here, let
him get him out of this worlde. And yet,
whatsoeuer shal mischaunce vnto vs two,
yours shoulde be but the one halfe thereof,
the greater parte I will alwaies take vn=
to mine owne selfe. So that if anie good
thing

thing doe happen vnto vs oure pleasure
shall be dubble if anye euill betide vs, you
shall haue but the one halfe of the griefe,
and I the other. As for my selfe, if God so
woulde, it were vnto me a pleasure, euen
to ende my life in your armes. Ma. Men
can better sustaine and beare with ᵭ which
chaunceth according to the common course
and rule of nature. For I see that some parentes are more troubled wyth their chil-
drens euill manners, than with their naturall deathes. Pam. To preuent such
misfortune, that it happen not vnto vs, it
resteth for the most part in our power: Ma.
How so? Pam. For commonly parentes,
which bee good and vertuous, haue good ᵭ
vertuous childen, I meane as concerning
their natural disposition, for doues do not
hatch Puthockes: wherefore we will first
indeuour to bee good our selues, and oure
next care shall bee, that our childen may
euen from the mothers brest, be seasoned
with vertuous counsails, and right opinions, for it skilleth not a little what licour
you poure into a newe bessell at the first.
Finallye, we shall prouide that they may

C.ij.   haue

haue euen at home in our house a good example of lyfe to followe. Ma. Harde it is to bꝛing that to paſſe that you ſay. Pam. No maruaile, foꝛ commendable, and good it is. And foꝛ that alſo are you harde to bée entreated and wonne, the moꝛe deficile and harde it is, the moꝛe good will and indeuour ſhall wée put there vnto. Maria. You ſhall haue mée a matter ſoft and plyant, ſée you ẏ you do your part in foꝛming and ſhaping me as you ought. Pam. But in the meane while ſaye thoſe thꝛée woꝛdes which J require of you. Ma. Nothing were moꝛe eaſie foꝛ me to doe, but woꝛdes be wynged, and when they be flowen out once doe not retire, J will tell you what were a better way foꝛ vs both. You ſhall treate with your Parentes and myne, and with their will and conſent let the matter be concluded. Pam. Ah you ſet me to wooe againe, it is in you, with thꝛée woꝛds to diſpatch the whole matter. Ma. Whether it lyeth in mée ſo to doe (as you ſay) J knowe not, foꝛ J am not at liberty. And in olde time mariages were not concluded without the will ⁊ conſent of their

parents

340

Dialogues.

parents oz elders. But howsoeuer the case
be, I suppose our mariage shall bée the
moze luckie, if it be made by the authozitie
of our parents. And your part it is to seke
and craue the good will, foz vs to doe it, it
were vnséemelye: virginite would séeme
alwayes to be taken with violence, yea
though sometime we loue the partie most
earnestly. Pam. I wil not let to séeke their
good will, so that I may alwayes be in an
assurance of your consent. Ma. You néede
not doubt thereof, be of good chéere (my
Pamphile) Pam. You are herein moze
scrupulus yet then I woulde with you to
be. Ma. Nay marie, waye, and consider
you well with your selfe, befoze, wherbn-
to you haue set your minde and will. And
do not take into your counsaile, this blind
affection bozne towardes my person, but
rather reason, foz that which affection de-
cerneth is liked foz a ceasō, but that which
reason auiseth is neuer mislyked. Pam.
Certes thou speakest like a wittie wench;
wherefoze I intende to followe thy counsayle. Ma. You shall not repent you thereof, but howbe sirha there is now fallen in-

C.iij.   to

341

to my minde a doubt , which vexeth mæ
soze. Pam. Away with all such doubtes
foz Gods sake . Ma. Why will you haue
me marry my selfe to a dead man . Pam.
Not so,foz I will reuiue againe. Maria.
Now,loc you haue boided this doubt,fare
yœ well my *Pamphile*. Pam. Sœ you I
pzay that I may so doe . Ma. I pzay God
giue you a good night , why fetch you such
a sighe man ? Pam. A good night say you?
I woulde to God you would vouchsafe to
giue me that , which you wishe mœ . Ma.
Soft andfairz, I pzay you your harnest is
as yet but in the grœne blade. Pam. Shall
I haue nothing of yours wyth me at my
beparture . Ma Take this Pomander to
chœre your harte wyth . Pam. Yet giue
me a kisse withal I pzay thœ.Ma.I would
kœpe my birginitie whole , and bndcfiled
foz you . Pa. Why doth a kisse take ought
away from your birginitie ? Ma. Would
you thinke it well done that I shoulde be
frœ of kisses bnto other men . Pam. Nay
marrie I would haue my kisses spared foz
my selfe . Ma. I kœpe them foz you then.
And yet there is an other thing in y way,
                                    which

Dialogues.

which maketh me that I dare not at thys
time giue you a kiſſe. Pam. What is that.
Ma. You ſaye that your ſoule is alreadie
gone well néere altogither into my body,
and a very ſmall parte thereof taryeth behinde in your owne, ſo that I feare in time
of a kiſſe, that which remayneth might
happen to ſterte out after it, & then were
you altogither without a ſoule. Haue you
therefoꝛe my right hande in token of mutuall loue, and ſo fare you well. Go you
earneſtly about your matters. And I foꝛ
my part in the meane while, ſhall pꝛay
vnto Chꝛiſt, that the thing which
you do, may be vnto the ioy
and felicitie of vs
both. Amen

Of the yong man and the
euill disposed woman.

Lucrecia.　　　Sophronius.

IEsu mercy my olde lo-
uing Frynde *Sophronius*,
are you at length come a-
gaine vnto vs? nowe mee
thinkes you haue béene a-
waye euen a worlde space,
Truelye at the first blushe I scarce knewe
you. Sophronius. And why so myne olde
acquaintaunce *Lucres*? Lucres. Why so?
bicause at your departing you had no berd
at al, now you become a handsome beardling. But what is the matter my swéete
harte: for me thinks you are waxed more
sterne and graue countenaunced then to
fore you had wont. Sophronius. I would
gladly talke with you friendlye in some
place aparte from all companye. Lucres.
Why are we not here alone (my luste?)
Sophronius. No, let vs go our selues into
some place yet more secret and priuie. Lu.
Be it so, let vs go into my inwarde cham-
ber,

ber, if ought you lift to doe. Sophronius. Yet mee thinketh this place is not close & secret ynough. Lucres. Why? whence comes this new shamefastnesse vpon you. I haue a Closet wherein I lay vp my Iewels and array, a place so darke that vnneth the one of vs shall see the other. So. Looke round about it, if there be any crany or rifte. Lu. Here is not a cranye nor rifte to be seene. So. Is there no body neere that mought listen and here vs? Lu. No verily not a flie (my ioy) why doubt you? why go you not about your purpose? So. Shall wee here beguile the eies of God? Lu. Not so, for he seeth thorow all things? So. Or shall wee be out of the sight of his Aungels? Lu. Neyther, for no bodie can hide him out of their sight. So. How happeneth it then, that we be not ashamed to doe that before the eies of God, and in the presence of his holy Aungels, which wee woulde be ashamed to doe in the syght of men? Lu. What a strange thing is this, came you hither to preache? put yee on, one of Saint Frances cowles, and get ye vp into the Pulpit, and let vs heare you

there

Dialogues.

there my yong Beardling. So. Neither
would I thinke it much so to doe,if by that
meane I might call you backe from thys
kind of life , not only most foule & shameful,but also most miserable. Lu. And why
so good sir? I must get my liuing one way
oz other,euery man liueth and is maintai-
ned by his craft,& science, this is our trade
our lands and reuenues. So. I would to
God (good friende *Lucres*) that you , voy-
ding foz a while this dzonkennesse of the
mynde, coulde finde in your heart rightly
to ponder and consider with me, the thing
as it is . Lu. Keepe your sermond till an
other time , nowe let vs take our pleasure
(my good friende *Sophronie*) So. All that
you doe, you doe it foz lucre and gaines I
am sure.Lu. Therin you haue gone nere
the marke. So. Well,you shall lose no
parte of that, which you make your accompt vppon, I will giue you euen foure
times as much onely,to lend me your attentiue care. Lu. Say on then euen what
you please. So. First aunswere me to this.
Haue you any that beareth you euill wil?
Lu. No then one . So. And are there not
                                            some

347

some againe, whome you hate likewise:
Lu. Euen as they deserue at my hande.
So. Now if it lay in thée to pleasure them
wouldest thou in faith do it: Lu. Nay so
ner woulde I giue them their bane. So.
Uerie well, consider now, consider I saye
whither ought thou mayest doe to them
moꝛe pleasaunt and better lyked, then to
let them sée thée leade this maner of lyfe,
so shamefull and wꝛetched. On the other
side, what canst thou do moꝛe to the griefe
and missliking of them, which be thy verye
friendes in déde: Lu. Such was my lot,
and destinie. So. Moꝛeouer, that which is
compted to be the most harde, and heauie
happe of those which are cast out into I-
lands, oꝛ banished vnto the people most in
humaine and barbarous, the same haue
you of your owne frée will, and election,
taken vnto your selfe. Lu. And what is
that: So. Hast not thou of thine accoꝛde
renounced & foꝛsaken all naturall affections and loues, your father, mother, bꝛe-
thꝛen, sistrene, aunt, great aunt, & whom-
soeuer besside nature hath linked vnto thée
foꝛ they in vaye déde, are full euill ashamed

med of thée, and thou darest not once come into their sight. Lu. Naye marrye, mée thinkes I haue luckilye chaunged myne affectes, in that for a few louers, nowe I haue won me verie many, among whome you are one, whome I haue accompted off as my naturall brother. So. Let passe this light accustomed talke, & way the matter as it is, in earnest. And first beléeue mée this (my *Lucres*) shée that hath so many louers, hath no loue at all. They that resort vnto thée, doe not take thée for their loue, but rather for their luste, sée howe thou hast debased thy selfe wretched Woman. Christ helde thée so déere, that hée vouchsafed to redéeme thée with his most precious bloud, to the ende, thou mightest partake with him in his heauenlye kingdome. And thou makest thy selfe a cōmon Gonge, or muckhill wherevnto fowle and filthy, scalde, and scuruie, doth at their pleasure resort, to shake off their filth and corruption. That if thou be yet frée and not infected wyth that lothsome kinde of leprie, commonly called the french pockes, assure thy selfe thou cannot long be wyth-

out

out it. Which if it chaunce thée to haue,
what in moze miserable and wzetched case
then thou, yea, though other things were
as thou wouldst wish (J meane) thy sub=
stance and fame, what shalt thou then be,
but a lump of quick carraine:you thought
it a great matter to be obedient vnto your
mother,now you liue in scruitude , vnder
a filthie bawde. It went to your heart to
heare the good aduertisements of your fa=
ther, here you must often tymes take in
good parte,euen the stripes of dzonkardes,
and madbzaines , you coulde awaye with
no maner of wozke, when you were with
your friendes, to helpe towardes your ly=
uing,but in this place what trouble,what
continuall watcking are you faine to sus=
taine ? Lu. From whence(and God will)
coms this new pzating pzeacher.So.Now
J pzaye thée , haue this also in thy minde.
The flower of beautie , which is the baite
that allureth men to loue thée , in shozte
time it shall fade , and decaye, And what
shalt thou then doe , vnhappie creature,
what donghill shall be moze vile,and vn=
regarded than thou then ? than loe , thou
shalt

Dialogues.

ſhalt of an hoꝛe, become a bawde, yet eue⸗
ry one of you commeth not vnto that pꝛo⸗
motion, but if that befalleth thee, what is
moꝛe abhominable; oꝛ neuer repꝛocheth e⸗
uen to the wicked occupacion of the deuill.
Lu. Truth it is in good faith, *Sophronie* in
a maner all that you haue hitherto ſayde.
But howe commeth this newe holineſſe
vpon you, who were wont to be amongſt
all the little gods, yet one of the leaſt, foꝛ
no man repaired hither, eyther oftener oꝛ
at moꝛe vntimely howꝛes, than your ſelf?
I heare ſay you haue béene at Rome late⸗
lie. So. I haue ſo in déede. Lucres. Why
men are wont to come from thence woꝛſe
than they went thither. How happeneth
the contrarie to you? So I will tell you,
bycauſe I went not to Rome, with that
minde, and after that ſoꝛt, other common⸗
lie goe to Rome, euen of ſet purpoſe to re⸗
tourne woꝛſe, ⁊ ſo doing they want none
occaſions when they come there, to be as
they purpoſed. But I went thither in the
companie of an honeſt vertuous man, by
whoſe aduiſe, in ſtéede of a bibbing bottel,
I caried with me, a handſome little booke
the

the new testament of *Erasmus* translation.
Lu. Of *Erasmus*? And they saye he is an
heretike and an halfe. So. Why hath the
name of that man come hither also? Lu.
None more famous with vs. So. Haue
you euer seene his persone? Lu. Neuer,
but in good fayth I woulde I might, bycause I haue hearde so much euill of hym.
So. Perhaps of them that be euill themselues. Lu. Nay truely, euen of reuerend
personages. So. What be they. Lucres.
I may not tell you that. So. And why so
I pray. Lu. Bicause if you should blab it
out, and it come vnto their eares. I should
lose no small part of my lyuing. So.
Feare thou not, thou shalt speake it to a
stone. Lu. Harken hither in thine eare the,
So. A fonde wench, what needeth it to
lay mine eare to thine, seing we be alone?
except it were that God shoulde not heare
it. Oh lyuing God, I see thou art a religious whore, thou doest thy charity vpon
Mendicants. Lu. Well, I get more by
these Mendicants & simple beggers, than
by you riche folke. So. So I thinke, they
spoyle and prowle from honest matrones
to

Mendicant.
Friers.

Dialogues.

to cast at whores tayles. Lu. But tell on
your tale concerning the booke. So. I will
so doe, and better it is. Therein Paule
taught me a lesso, who being indued with
the spirite of truth could not lie, that neyther whores, nor whore haunters shall
inherite the kingdome of heauen. When
I had reade this, I beganne to consider
with my selfe in this wise. It is a small
thinge, which I looke to be heire of by my
father, and yet neuerthelesse rather I had
to shake hands with all wanton women,
then to be set beside that inheritance, how
muche more then doth it sit me on, to beware ý my father in heauē doth not disinherite me of that far more excellent inheritance, for against mine earthly father,
which goeth about to disinherite me, or to
cast me off, the ciuill lawes doe offer a remedie, but if God list to cast of, or disinherite, there is no helpe at all. Wherevpon,
I forthwith vtterlie forsended my selfe,
the vse and familiaritie of all euill disposed women. Lu. That is if you be able to
lyue chaste. So. It is a good parte of the
bertue of continencie, hartilie to couit and

D.j.   desirs

353

desire the same, if it will not so bée, well, the vttermoſt remedie is to take a Wife. When I was come to Rome, I powred out the hole ſincke of my conſcience into the boſome of a certayne Frier penitenti- arie, who with many words, right wiſe- lye exhorted mœ to puritie, and cleanneſſe of minde and bodye, and vnto the deuout reading of holie ſcripture, with oft prayer & ſoberneſſe of life, for my penaunce he en- ioyned me naught elſe, but that I ſhoulde knœle on my knées before the high alter, and ſay ẏ Pſalme *Miſerere mei deus.* And if I had mony to giue in almoys vnto ſome poore bodie a *Carolyne.* And wheras I mer- uayled much, that for ſo many times, as I hadde confeſſed my ſelfe to haue played the brothell, he layed vppon me ſo ſmall a penaunce, hée aunſwered me right plea- ſauntlye thus. Sonne (quoth he) if thou truely repent, if thou change thy conuer- ſation, I paſſe not on thy penance, but if thou procœd ſtil therin, thy very luſt it ſelf ſhal at the length bring thée to paine and penaunce ynough I warrant thée, though the Prieſt appointeth thée none, for exam- ple

ple loke vpon my selfe, whome thou seest now, bleare eyed, palsey shaken, and croked, and in time paste I was euen such a one as thou declarest thy selfe to be. Thus loe haue I learned to leaue it. Lu. Why then for ought that I can see I haue loste my *Sophronius*. So. Nay rather thou hast him safe, for before he was in deede loste, as one which neyther loued thee nor hymselfe. He now loueth thee with a true loue, and thristeth thy saluation. Lu. What aduise you me then to doe, friende *Sophronius?* So. As sonne as possible you may to withdrawe your selfe from this kinde of lyfe, you are yet but a girle (to speake off) and the spot of your misdemeanour maye be washed away. Either take an husband (so doing we wyll contribute some thing to preferre you) eyther else get you into some godly Colledge or Monestery which receyueth those that haue done amisse, vpon promise of amendment, or at the leastwyse departing from this place, betake your selfe into the seruice of some vertuous and well disposed Matrone. And to which of these you liste to enclyne your minde;

minde, J offer you my friendly helpe and furtheraunce. Lu. Now J besech you with all my hart *Sophronie* looke about & prouide for me, J will follow your counsayle. So. But in the meane while conuey your selfe from out of this place. Lu. Alack so sone, So. Why not, rather this day than to morow: namely since lingering it is damage, and delay is daungerous. Lu. Whether should J then repaire, where should J stay my selfe? So. You shall packe vp all your apparell and Jewels, & deliuer it vnto me in the euening, my seruaunt shall closely carrie it, vnto a faithfull honest Matrone. And within a while after, J will leade you out, as it were to walke with me and you shal secretly abide in that Matrons house, at my charge, vntill J prouide for you: And that time shall not bæ long. Lu.

Be it so my *Sophronius*, J betake
my selfe wholy vnto you.
So. For so doing here
after, you shall
haue ioy.

FINIS.

The diſcouerie
of witchcraft,

Wherein the lewde dealing of witches
and witchmongers is notablie detected, the
knauerie of coniurors, the impietie of inchan-
tors, *the follie of ſoothſaiers, the impudent falſ-*
hood of couſenors, the infidelitie of atheiſts,
the peſtilent practiſes of Pythoniſts, the
curioſitie of figurecaſters, the va-
nitie of dreamers, the begger-
lie art of Alcu-
myſtrie,

The abhomination of idolatrie, the hor-
rible art of poiſoning, the vertue and power of
naturall magike, and all the conueiances
of Legierdemaine and iuggling are deciphered:
and many other things opened which
haue long lien hidden, howbeit
verie neceſſarie to
be knowne.

Heerevnto is added a treatiſe vpon the
nature and ſubſtance of ſpirits and diuels,
&c : all latelie written
by Reginald Scot
Eſquire.

1. Iohn. 4, 1.

Beleeue not euerie ſpirit, but trie the ſpirits, whether they are
of God; for manie falſe prophets are gone
out into the world, &c.

1584

357

uerie and deceipts wherevpon this art dependeth, whereby the readers maie be more delighted in reading, than the practisers benefited in simplie vsing the same. For it is an art consisting wholie of subtiltie and deceipt, whereby the ignorant and plaine minded man through his too much credulitie is circumuented, and the humor of the other slie cousener satisfied.

A notable storie written by Erasmus of two Alcumysts, also of longation and curtation.

The fist Chapter.

He thirdexample is reported by Erasmus, whose excellent learning and wit is had to this daie in admiration. He in a certeine dialog intituled *Alcumystica* doth finelie bewraie the knauerie of this craftie art; wherein he proposeth one Balbiné, a verie wise, learned, and deuout preest, howbeit such a one as was bewitched, and mad vpon the art of Alcumystrie. Which thing another cousening preest perceiued, and dealt with him in maner and forme following.

Eraf. in col-loq. de arte alcumystica.

M.Doctor Balbine (said he) I being a stranger vnto you maie seeme verie saucie to trouble your worship with my bold sute, who alwaies are busied in great and diuine studies. To whome Balbine, being a man of few words, gaue a nodde: which was more than he vsed to euerie man. But the preest knowing his humor, said; I am sure sir, if you knew my sute, you would pardon mine importunitie. I praie thee good sir Iohn (said Balbine) shew me thy mind, and be breefe. That shall I do sir (said he) with a good will. You know M.Doctor, through your skill in philosophie, that euerie mans destinie is not alike; and I for my part am at this point, that I cannot tell whether I maie be counted happie or infortunate. For when I weigh mine owne case, or rather my state, in part I seeme fortunate, and in part miserable. But Balbine being a man of some surlinesse, alwaies willed him to draw his matter to a more compendious forme: which thing the preest said

A flattering & clawing preamble.

faid he would do, and could the better perfozme; bicaufe Balbine himfelfe was fo learned and expert in the verie matter he had to repeat, and thus he began.

I haue had, euen from my childhod, a great felicitie in the art of Alcumystrie, which is the verie marrow of all philofophie. Balbine at the naming of the word Alcumystrie, inclined and yeelded himfelfe moze attentiuelie to hearken vnto him: marie it was onelie in gefture of bodie; foz he was fpare of fpéech, and yet he bad him pzocéed with his tale. Then faid the pzéeft, Wretch that I am, it was not my lucke to light on the beft waie: foz you M. Balbine know (being fo vniuerfallie learned) that in this art there are two waies, the one called longation, the other curtation; and it was mine ill hap to fall vpon longation. When Balbine afked him the difference of thofe two waies; Oh fir faid the pzéeft, you might count me impudent, to take vpon me to tell you, that of all other are beft learned in this art, to whome I come, moft humblie to beféech you to teach me that luckie waie of curtation. The cunninger you are, the moze eaflie you maie teach it me: and therefoze hide not the gift that God hath giuen you, from your bzother, who maie perifh foz want of his defire in this behalfe; and doubtleffe Iefus Chzift will inrich you with greater bleffings and endowments.

Balbine being abafhed partlie with his impoztunitie, and partlie with the ftrange circumftance, told him that (in truth) he neither knew what longation oz curtation meant; and therefoze required him to expound the nature of thofe wozds. Well (quoth the pzéeft) fince it is your pleafure, I will do it, though I fhall thereby take vpon me to teach him that is indéed much cunninger than my felfe. And thus he began: Oh fir, they that haue fpent all the daies of their life in this diuine facultie, do turne one nature and fozme into another, two waies, the one is verie bzéefe, but fomewhat dangerous; the other much longer, marie verie fafe, fure, and commodious. Howbeit, I thinke my felfe moft vnhappie that haue fpent my time and trauell in that waie which vtterlie miffiketh me, and neuer could get one to fhew me the other that I fo earneftlie defire. And now I come to your wozfhip, whom I know to be wholie learned and expert herein, hoping that you will (foz charities fake) comfoztt your bzother, whofe

Longation and curtation in Alcumystrie.

Note how the coufener circumuenteth Balbine.

whose felicitie and well doing now resteth onelie in your hands; and therefoze I beséech you reléeue me with your counsell.

By these and such other wozds when this cousening varlot had auoided suspicion of guile, and assured Balbine that he was perfect and cunning in the other waie: Balbine his fingers itched, and his hart tickled; so as he could hold no longer, but burst out with these wozds: Let this curtation go to the diuell, whose name I did neuer so much as once heare of befoze, and therefoze doo much lesse vnderstand it. But tell me in good faith, doo you exactlie vnderstand longation? Pea said the pzeest, doubt you not hereof: but I haue no fansie to that waie, it is so tedious. Why (quoth Balbine) what time is required in the accomplishment of this wozke by waie of longation? Too too much said the Alcumyster, euen almost a whole yéere: but this is the best, the surest, and the safest waie, though it be foz so manie moneths pzolonged, befoze it yéeld aduantage foz cost and charges expended thereabouts. Set your hart at rest (said Balbine) it is no matter, though it were two yéeres, so as you be well assured to bzing it then to passe.

Faire words make fooles faine, and large offers blind the wise.

Finallie, it was there and then concluded, that presentlie the pzeest should go in hand with the wozke, and the other should beare the charge, the gaines to be indifferentlie diuided betwixt them both, and the wozke to be doone pziuilie in Balbins house. And after the mutuall oth was taken foz silence, which is vsuall and requisite alwaies in the beginning of this mysterie; Balbine deliuered monie to the Alcumpster foz bolles, glasses, coles, &c: which should serue foz the erection and furniture of the fozge. Which monie the Alcumpster had no sooner fingered, but he ran merilie to the dice, to the alehouse, & to the stewes, and who there so lustie as cousening sir Iohn: who indéed this waie made a kind of alcumpsticall transfozmation of monie. Now Balbine vzged him to go about his businesse, but the other told him, that if the matter were once begun, it were halfe ended: foz therein consisted the greatest difficultie.

Well, at length he began to furnish the foznace, but now foz-sooth a new supplie of gold must be made, as the séed and spawne of that which must be ingendzed and grow out of this wozke of Alcumpstrie. Foz euen as a fish is not caught without a bait, no mozke moze is gold multiplied without ſome parcels of gold : and therfoze gold muſt be the foundation and groundwozke of that art, oz elſe all the fat is in the fier. But all this while Balbine was occupied in calculating, and muſing vpon his accompt; caſting by arythmetike, how that if one ownce yelded fifteene, then how much gaines two thouſand ownces might yeld : foz ſo much he determined to emploie that waie.

When the Alcumpſt had alſo conſumed this monie, ſhewing great trauell a moneth oz twaine, in placing the bellowes, the coles, and ſuch other ſtuffe, and no whit of pzofit pzoceding oz comming thereof : Balbine demanded how the wozld went, our Alcumpſt was as a man amazed. Howbeit he ſaid at length; Fozſooth euen as ſuch matters of impoztance commonlie doo go fozward, wherunto there is alwaies verie difficult acceſſe. There was (ſaith he) a fault (which I haue now found out) in the choice of the coles, which were of oke, and ſhould haue bene of beech. One hundzeth duckets were ſpent that waie, ſo as the diſting houſe and the ſtewes were partakers of Balbines charges. But after a new ſupplie of monie, better coles were pzouided, and matters moze circumſpectlie handled. Howbeit, when the foʒge had trauelled long, and bzought foozth nothing, there was another excuſe found out; to wit, that the glaſſes were not tempered as they ought to haue bene. But the moze monie was diſburſed hereabouts, the wozſſe willing was Balbine to giue ouer, accozding to the diſers veine, whome fruteleſſe hope bzingeth into a fooles paradiſe.

The Alcumpſt, to caſt a good colour vpon his knauerie, tooke on like a man mooneſicke, and pzofeſſed with great wozds full of foʒgerie and lies, that he neuer had ſuch lucke befoze. But hauing found the errer, he would be ſure enough neuer hereafter to fall into the like ouerſight, and that hencefozward all ſhould be ſafe and ſure, and thzoughlie recompenſed in the end with large increaſe. Herevpon the wozkehouſe is now the third time repaired, and a new ſupplie yet once againe put into the Alcumpſts hand; ſo as the glaſſes were changed. And now at length the Alcumpſt vttered another point of his art and cunning to Balbine; to wit, that thoſe matters would pzoceed much better, if he ſent our Ladie a few French crownes in reward: foz the art being

being holie, the matter cannot prosperouslp proceed, without the
fauour of the saints. Which counsell exceedinglie pleased Balbine, who was so deuout and religious, that no daie escaped him but he said our Ladie mattens.

Now our Alcumpster hauing receiued the offering of monie,
goeth on his holie pilgrimage, euen to the next village, & there
consumeth it euerie penie, among bawds and knaues. And at
his returne, he told Balbine that he had great hope of good lucke
in his businesse; the holie virgine gaue such fauourable countenance, and such attentiue care vnto his praiers and vowes. But
after this, when there had béene great trauell bestowed, and not a
dram of gold yéelded nor leuied from the forge; Balbine began
to expostulate and reason somewhat roundlie with the cousening
fellowe; who still said he neuer had such filthie lucke in all his life
before, and could not deuise by what meanes it came to passe, that
things went so ouerthwartlie. But after much debating betwixt
them vpon the matter, at length it came into Balbines head to
aske him if he had not foreslowed to heare masse, or to saie his
houres: which if he had done, nothing could prosper vnder his
hand. Without doubt (said the cousener) you haue hot the naile
on the head. Wretch that I am! I remember once or twise being at a long feast, I omitted to saie mine *Aue Marie* after dinner. So so (said Balbine) no maruell then that a matter of such
importance hath had so euill successe. The Alcumpster promised
to do penance; as to heare twelue masses for two that he had
foreslowed; and for euerie *Aue* ouerslipped, to render and repeate twelue to our Ladie.

Soone after this, when all our Alcumpsters monie was spent,
& also his shifts failed how to come by any more, he came home
with this deuise, as a man wonderfullie fraied and amazed, pitiouslie crieng and lamenting his misfortune. Whereat Balbine being astonished, desired to knowe the cause of his complaint. Oh (said the Alcumpster) the courtiers haue spied our enterprise; so as I for my part looke for nothing but present imprisonment. Whereat Balbine was abashed, bicause it was flat
fellonie to go about that matter, without speciall licence. But
(quoth the Alcumpster) I feare not to be put to death, I would it
would fall out so: marrie I feare least I shall be shut vp in some
castell

caftell oʒ towʒe,and there ſhall be foʒced to tug about this woʒke and bʒoile in this buſineſſe all the daies of my life.

Now the matter being bʒought to conſultation , Balbine, bſcauſe he was cunning in the art of rhetoʒike , and not altogither ignoʒant in lawe,beat his bʒaines in deuiſing how the accuſation might be anſwered, and the danger auoided. Alas (ſaid the Alcumpſter) you trouble your ſelfe all in vaine ,foʒ you ſée the crime is not to be denied, it is ſo generallie bʒuted in court : nether can the fact be defended, bicauſe of the manifeſt lawe publiſhed againſt it . To be ſhoʒt, when manie waies were deuiſed, and diuerſe excuſes alledged by Balbine, and no ſure ground to ſtand on foʒ their ſecuritie;at length the Alcumpſter hauing pʒeſent want and néd of monie, framed his ſpéech in this ſoʒt ; Sir ſaid he to Balbine, we vſe ſlowe counſell, and yet the matter requireth haſt. Foʒ I thinke they are comming foʒ me yer this time to hale me awaie to pʒiſon ; and I ſée no remedie but to die valiantlie in the cauſe. In good faith (ſaid Balbine) I knowe not what to ſaie to the matter. No moʒe do I ſaid the Alcumpſter,but that I ſée theſe courtiers are hungrie foʒ monie, and ſo much the readier to be coʒrupted & framed to ſilence. And though it be a hard matter, to giue thoſe rakehels till they be ſatisſied : yet I ſée no better counſell oʒ aduiſe at this time . No moʒe could Balbine, who gaue him ſhirtie ducats of gold to ſtop their mouthes, who in an honeſt cauſe would rather haue giuen ſo manie téeth out of his head, than one of thoſe péeces out of his pouch. This coine had the Alcumpſter, who foʒ all his pʒetenſes & gaie gloſes was in no danger, other than foʒ lacke of monie to léeſe his lemon oʒ concubine, whoſe acquaintance he would not giue ouer, noʒ foʒbeare hir companie,foʒ all the goods that he was able to get,were it by neuer ſuch indirect dealing and vnlawfull meanes.

Well, yet now once againe doth Balbine newlie furniſh the foʒge,a pʒaier being made befoʒe to our Ladie to bleſſe the enterpʒiſe. And all things being pʒouided and made readie accoʒding to the Alcumpſters owne aſking, & all neceſſaries largelie miniſtred after his owne liking ; a whole yeare being likewiſe now conſumed about this bootleſſe buſineſſe, and nothing bʒought to paſſe ;there fell out a ſtrange chance, and that by this meanes inſuing, as you ſhall heare.

Our

Marke how this Alcumyſter goeth frō one degree of couſenage to another.

Our Alcumpſter foꝛſooth vſed a little extraoꝛdinarie lewd cõpanie with a courtiers wiſe, whiles he was from home, who ſuſpecting the matter, came to the dooꝛe vnlocked foꝛ, and called to come in, thꝛeatning them that he would bꝛeake open the dooꝛes vpon them. Some pꝛeſent deuiſe (you ſée) was now requiſite, and there was none other to be had, but ſuch as the opoꝛtunitie offered; to wit, to leape out at a backe window: which he did, not without great hazard, and ſome hurt. But this was ſoone blazed abꝛoad, ſo as it came to Balbines eare, who ſhewed in countenance that he had heard héereof, though he ſaid nothing. But the Alcumpſter knew him to be deuout, & ſomewhat ſuperſtitious: and ſuch men are eaſie to be intreated to foꝛgiue, how great ſoeuer the fault be, and deuiſed to open the matter in maner and foꝛme following.

The mildeſt and ſofteſt nature is cõmonlie ſooneſt abuſed.

O Loꝛd (ſaith he befoꝛe Balbine) how infoꝛtunatlie goeth our buſineſſe foꝛward! I maruell what ſhould be the cauſe. Whereat Balbine, being one otherwiſe that ſéemed to haue vowed ſilence, tooke occaſion to ſpeake, ſaieng; It is not hard to knowe the impediment and ſtop héereof: foꝛ it is ſinne that hindereth this matter; which is not to be dealt in but with pure hands. Whereat the Alcumpſter fell vpon his knées, beating his bꝛeaſt, & lamentablie cried, ſaieng; Oh maiſter Balbine, you ſaie moſt trulie, it is ſinne that hath doone vs all this diſpleaſure; not your ſinne ſir, but mine owne, good maiſter Balbine. Neither will I be aſhamed to diſcouer my filthineſſe vnto you, as vnto a moſt holy and ghoſtlie father. The infirmitie of the fleſh had ouercome me, and the diuell had caught me in his ſnare. Oh wꝛetch that I am! Of a pꝛéeſt I am become an adulterer, Howbeit, the monie that erſtwhile was ſent to our Ladie, was not vtterlie loſt: foꝛ if ſhe had not béene, I had certeinlie béene ſlaine. Foꝛ the good man of the houſe bꝛake open the dooꝛe, and the windowe was leſſe than I could get out thereat. And in that extremitie of danger it came into my mind to fall downe pꝛoſtrate to the virgine; beſéeching hir (if our gift were acceptable in hir ſight) that ſhe would, in conſideration thereof, aſſiſt me with hir helpe. And to be ſhoꝛt, I ran to the windowe, and found it bigge enough to leape out at. Which thing Balbine did not onelie beléeue to be true, but in reſpect therof foꝛgaue him, religiouſlie admoniſhing him

En immenſæ caui ſpirant mendacia folles.

365

him to ſhew himſelfe thankfull to that pitifull and bleſſed Ladie.

Now once againe moze is made a new ſuplie of monie, and mutuall pzomiſe made to handle this diuine matter hence fozward purelie and holilie. To be ſhozt, after a great number of ſuch parts plaied by the Alcumyſter; one of Balbins acquaintance eſpied him, that knew him from his childhod to be but a couſening merchant; and told Balbine what he was, and that he would handle him in the end, euen as he had vſed manie others: foz a knaue he euer was, and ſo he would pzoue. But what did Balbine, thinke you? Did he complaine of this counterfet, oz cauſe him to be puniſhed? No, but he gaue him monie in his purſſe, and ſent him awaie; deſiring him, of all courteſie, not to blab abzoad how he had couſened him. And as foz the knaue Alcumyſter, he néeded not care who knew it, oz what came of it: foz he had nothing in goods oz fame to be loſt. And as foz his cunning in Alcumyſtrie, he had as much as an aſſe. By this diſcourſe Eraſmus would giue vs to note, that vnder the golden name of Alcumyſtrie there lieth lurking no ſmall calamitie; wherein there be ſuch ſeuerall ſhifts and ſutes of rare ſubtilties and deceipts, as that not onelie welthie men are thereby manie times impoueriſhed, and that with the ſwéete allurement of this art, thzough their owne couetouſneſſe; as alſo by the flattering baits of hoped gaine: but euen wiſe and learned men hereby are ſhamefullie ouerſhot, partlie foz want of due experience in the wiles and ſubtilties of the wozld, and partlie thzough the ſoftneſſe and pliablenes of their god nature, which couſening knaues do commonlie abuſe to their owne luſt and commoditie, and to the others vtter vndoing.

Balbine is aſhamed that he ſhould be ouerſhot and ouerſéene in a caſe of flat couſenage.